FISHING SEASON

FISHING SEASON

PHILIP WEIGALL

EXISLE
PUBLISHING

First published 2009

Exisle Publishing Limited
'Moonrising', Narone Creek Road, Wollombi, NSW 2325, Australia
P.O. Box 60–490, Titirangi, Auckland 0642, New Zealand
www.exislepublishing.com

National Library of Australia Cataloguing-in-Publication Data:

Weigall, Philip.

Fishing season / Philip Weigall.

ISBN 9781921497230 (hbk.)

Fly fishing.
Short stories.

A823.3

Designed by saso content & design pty ltd
Typeset in Adobe Caslon 11/16 by 1000 Monkeys Typesetting Services
Printed in China through Colorcraft Limited, Hong Kong

10 9 8 7 6 5 4 3 2 1

To my dear boys Daniel and Sean,
wishing you many happy seasons.

CONTENTS

Summer

Autumn

PREFACE

LIKE RISE, NYMPH and dry, in the language of flyfishing the word 'season' takes on a few meanings. Sometimes it simply describes the period when certain species may legally be fished for. Another usage is to define when a particular type of fishing is prevalent, say, mayfly season or grasshopper season. Season can even be used in place of 'fishing year', as in 'last season' or 'this coming season'. This definition is often employed when reflecting on a mistake or misfortune in the past, with a promise to correct it in the future.

In this book, the structure revolves around a fourth definition of season, being the passage of twelve months marked by a migrating sun, changes in the weather and, in the higher latitudes at least, the quarters of winter, spring, summer and autumn. During most of my fishing adventures (and I'm sure yours too) the season in this context is, at a minimum, the canvas on which the events are drawn. At other times, the season dominates to the extent that it pretty much is the story, and the incidents occurring around it are almost secondary.

The relationship between the seasons and flyfishing really struck me when looking back through some of my magazine columns, and proved the inspiration to put this book together. Some of the tales that follow have appeared in these columns, at least in part.

So this book is a journey through a fishing season, or should I say fishing *seasons*, as the events take place from the present back over 30 years and more. There are hot days and cold, the hard days and easy, the victories and defeats, people and places. Maybe more than anything else, this book is about all those small things that make flyfishing a life sport, which leave me as smitten with it now as I was in the beginning.

WINTER

INSTINCT

PETER JULIAN AND I go back as far as my first fly rod. When I was about ten years old Dad and I befriended Peter, his brother David and father John. At the time John and Peter (and to a lesser extent David) flyfished, while Dad and I used bait and spinners. I was catching my share of trout on little Celta lures, and grasshoppers and mudeyes drifted down the current beneath bubble floats. Flyfishing seemed like an interesting but unnecessarily elaborate way to snare a fish.

Nevertheless, from time to time I picked up my fly rod and had a go. I still have that rod, a 9-foot 7-weight fibreglass model that was (and is) very difficult to use. Somehow I persevered with it, catching the odd trout that forgave my short, sloppy presentations. But I always fell back to the reliable spinning rod when things became difficult.

Fishing my Celtas and Floppys, I kept up with Peter most of the time, catching as many if not more fish. However, Peter and his fly rod dominated in two important areas: he caught bigger trout than me, and he caught trout during the frantic evening rise. During this rise, when as many trout as we ever saw dotted the water with their swirls and slashes, the spinner was the most abject of failures. In the course of the dozens of these rises that Peter and I fished together, fly versus spinner, I can't recall catching a single trout. In hindsight some must have actually dodged the treble hooks, otherwise I would have eventually foul-hooked one.

It would be exaggerating to suggest Peter taught me to flyfish — there aren't too many adults who have the patience to instruct their friends in flyfishing, let alone kids. However, I could observe what Peter was doing. And occasionally, if he was feeling benevolent after a good session, he might take a few moments to show me a nail knot, or to recommend a Red Tag.

Over time my casting improved and so did the fly rods I used. Slowly, I began to catch trout. Most of my initial successes could be politely described as lucky — a trout on a drowned Royal Coachman that was hooked as I went to lift off; another as I was simply feeding a Matuka downstream without even casting. But then I began to catch trout more deliberately during the evening rise.

Finally, I caught some big ones. I recognised many of these latter fish as those that would merely 'follow' when spinning — the large trout that tantalised by chasing the lure to my feet without actually eating it. Decades later, I still marvel when a big trout follows my fly, then suddenly and gracefully engulfs it.

To my disappointment, I can't actually remember when it was or where that Peter and I finally went fishing together and I didn't at least bring the spinning rod along just in case. In any event our flyfishing trips together since are too many to recall. As I've spent the last couple of decades with flyfishing as my profession (to use the term loosely) as well as my passion, I've been able to close the skill gap between us. However, he still produces the odd surprise.

Which leads me to a recent winter trip to Tullaroop Reservoir, a large water storage in central Victoria less than an hour's drive north of my home. When levels are high, Tullaroop verges on attractive, with a mixture of grassy and timbered slopes framing fertile bays and corners. But after a few years of drought, the lake was low and stable, and kilometre after kilometre of the eastern shore was featureless. Well, featureless is a bit harsh. The water was pleasantly clear under a sunny mid-winter sky, and a narrow weedbed followed the shoreline contours. However, defined bays, inlets, sharp points, shallow flats or rocky headlands were non-existent. In other words, all the places one looks for inspiration when the trout become invisible were missing from a remarkably uniform shoreline.

Yet after half an hour of walking, chatting and throwing the odd aimless cast, Peter suddenly announced, 'I think I'll have a go here.' There was nothing at all to distinguish the spot from any other over the last kilometre. Just more rock and clay shoreline, sprinkled with the odd clump of winter-bleached grass, then just offshore a dark-brown weedbed perhaps half a rod broad dropping away into blue-green water beyond. Bidding Peter good luck, I continued. I half-heartedly set my sights on a group of skeletal drowned trees in the distance, but I hoped to see a trout move before then.

After I'd walked on for about five minutes, a cry of 'Whooo-eee!' carried on the light breeze. I looked back. In the middle distance, Peter's rod and posture had combined to adopt the question-mark shape of an angler hooked into something worthwhile. And although I was too far away to see detail, a large splash offshore confirmed he was into a good one.

Torn between the desire to catch one of my own and that almost childlike eagerness to see a big fish caught, I chose the latter course and gracefully jogged back to Peter in my clay-clogged waders. I arrived in time to witness the victorious beaching of a fat, silvery 4-pounder. Actually, I think Pete drew the fight out a little to make sure I experienced the full drama, but I guess that's a successful angler's prerogative.

The brown was a beauty, and when I looked closer there was a surprise. Firmly imbedded in the jaw scissors was a Bibio Hopper dry fly. An English loch-style dry in mid winter? Plainly, something a little spooky was going on here. Peter had not only stopped as if he'd hit a brick wall to cast over an essentially featureless spot, he had also taken the trouble to change to a pattern neither of us had previously even contemplated at Tullaroop, let alone in July. Yet soon after, he had caught a very nice trout.

Now, for the benefit of the scientifically minded, let's analyse what happened. We arrived at the lake late morning. I, admittedly, had fished it recently. Peter, however, hadn't visited Tullaroop for a few years, and then rarely on the east shore and never at that water level (fairly low). I had generously shared the benefit of my recent experience, suggesting a Tom Jones as a point fly and a small bead-head nymph on the dropper to imitate the abundant corixia. Peter had politely rigged up this way at first, but evidently, as soon as I was out of sight, he'd changed to a fly I hadn't even considered, let alone discussed. All this without an obvious reason to stop and fish in the first place.

Of course, I cross-examined Peter in an effort to uncover the *real* story behind his fine catch. Had he seen a fish rise? No. Had he seen a fish move? No. Had he imagined from a distance that he *might* have seen a fish move? No. Had he seen any insects on the surface? No. Had he spoken to anyone else recently about Tullaroop flies or hotspots? No. As a matter of fact, he didn't even know we were going there until that morning. 'Then why did you stop here and fish with that?' I asked with exasperation.

'I don't know,' Peter shrugged. 'It just felt like a good idea.'

It seems there are only two possibilities to explain Peter's success. One is sheer luck. Given our decades of friendly competition, this is a tempting explanation but, in this case, an unconvincing one. The other is instinct. Had Peter, by using what we sometimes think of as a sixth sense, known intuitively where to stop and what fly to use? That is certainly the more intriguing explanation.

This instinct thing is a source of fascination to me. When I'm having a good day, I sometimes anticipate a take to an invisible fly seconds before it actually happens. I can't *make* this feeling happen, but it's nice when it does. Another example is striking into a fish on a dark night, without really knowing why you struck in the first place.

Wild animals — including trout — clearly use instinct much more effectively than we do. Arguably, we modern-day humans retain the potential to use instinct effectively, but it seems that our ability to do so has largely been smothered by 21st-century life. We are now so insulated from the natural world that even extremes of weather which would have been lethal to our ancestors — like Victoria's snow-to-sea-level cold snap a couple of years back — are no more than an interesting novelty. The capacity to sense an impending blizzard in time to prepare fire and shelter no longer carries the life-saving benefits it once did. And if you don't use it perhaps you lose it.

I often find myself trying to explain to acquaintances (and sometimes even to myself) why fishing is so important in my life. A part of the reason is surely the opportunity to return once again to a place where instinct matters, where I can really use and test the wonderful intuitive abilities we are all born with — even if my fishing mates sometimes use those abilities better than I do ...

FIDDLER ON THE VISE

THE REST OF the family has turned in for an early night and the house is quiet. The fire crackles in the hearth, casting a flickering light on the leatherbound first editions in the bookcase. Ransome, Scholes, Ronalds ... A cold wind splatters rain on the study window, but you are warm and dry. A steaming coffee, fortified with a dash of single-malt scotch, waits patiently beside your right hand. Dire Straits play softly in the background, slightly muffled as the rain on the roof changes to sleet.

Although it's mid winter, your mind is five months in the future, visiting a mountain river in early summer. Dry-fly time, with long, warm days, clear water and gentle flows. Several patterns have proved indispensable during early summers past, however none more so than the Geehi Beetle. And not just any Geehi Beetle, but the one you tie with an extra-fat body and a short hackle. While it may not be the best floater, you have no doubt that trout are powerfully drawn to the half-drowned 'footprint' this fly leaves.

You open the top-left drawer of the desk, where temporarily redundant fly boxes rest, awaiting their season. Beside the box labelled '*Grasshoppers – Dry*', is the one you want: '*Beetles – Dry*'. Unexpectedly, seeing both boxes side-by-side causes you to revisit the confusion of a few summers ago, when an acquaintance insisted that the Geehi Beetle was, in fact, the best grasshopper fly he knew of. Then the moment passes, and you open the Beetle box, satisfied that the Geehi is correctly classified.

'Aha, just as I thought,' you murmur to yourself as you lift the lid. Two things are immediately obvious: there are only three Geehi Beetles left in their otherwise empty row; and all three are badly beaten up. Time to fix that.

The three survivors are pulled from the foam ridge. There is a moment of hesitation before you piff them into the wastepaper basket — after all, these flies served you well. But this is not the time for sentimentality. With the box now ready with an empty row, you begin.

First you reach for the bobbin, dangling from its hook on the wall. Then you open one of the little drawers in the timber box at the back of the desk, labelled '*Dry Fly #12*'. The Geehi works best in large sizes. A hook is fastened into the vise. Quick turns of thread with the bobbin make ready for the golden pheasant tail. The golden pheasant is clearly marked (of course) in the CD file that works perfectly for storing small packets of fly-tying materials. You're getting into a rhythm now and, with barely a pause, you pick a prime peacock quill from the canister beside the desk. A few herls later and the body is satisfactorily plump. Next the hackle — genetically grown, needless to say. These hackles are so long and easy to work with it almost feels like cheating. Almost.

In no time, the first Geehi is tied. A dab of lacquer behind the hook eye and it is on the foam drying row. You admire the new fly briefly, and then move on to the next. Like a machine, you produce fly after fly until, just as 'Water of Love' (appropriately) begins to play, the twelfth Geehi Beetle joins its companions.

There is a moment to lean forward and admire your work. After a slow sip of coffee, you ask yourself the hard question. Could any of those Geehis be better? Be honest now. But no, each one is perfect. Into the box they go.

You put the coffee down and notice that it is quiet outside. A glance at the window reveals that the sleet has turned to snow, settling on the sill. Shivering involuntarily, you get up from the chair and put another log on the fire. Now, how are the Red Tags ...?

The cat has been sick on the carpet, and your toddler is trying to find out how many pieces of Lego will fit in the DVD player slot, when you notice you are all out of Milly Midges. Your angling companion will be arriving in half an hour for a trip to the central highlands lakes. You sponge up the cat's mess, fighting the urge to make your own much larger contribution. For a moment your crowded mind calculates how old the cat is — shouldn't it be dead by now?

But the thought is interrupted by a strange whirring sound from the DVD player, and a delighted giggle from your two-year-old. Gently restraining child with one hand, and inspecting the *Any small fly I was too disorganised to put in the right box*-box, you look desperately for an alternative. The Shipmans perhaps, or those slightly worn-looking superglue buzzers. They'll do won't they? 'Yeah right,' says a voice of bitter experience from deep inside your head. If you don't have any Milly Midges, then guess which fly will be the only one the trout want?

With a reluctant acceptance of this reality, you distract your offspring with a giant toy caterpillar that talks in a slightly spooky Chinese–American accent, and sneak off to the study. Shoving a half-finished manuscript and some bills (about the same mass) to one side, you sit at the study desk and reach hopefully among the pile of opened packets in the hook drawer. Size 12 grub hooks are what you need and, eventually, in the morning's first small victory, you find the right packet — but then notice only two hooks are left. Never mind, you make a start anyway.

After a few false beginnings, the first Milly is almost finished. Perhaps it's a bit emaciated around the thorax but time is marching on. With some satisfaction, you make a final turn with the bobbin ... and the thread inexplicably snaps. The peacock herl springs gleefully from the hook, while the Hi-Vis gill appears to vaporise. Fingers stiffening with cold (keeping the study door shut also blocks the heat from the living room fire), you reach tiredly for more Hi-Vis and herl.

Three-quarters of the way through the second Milly, the toy caterpillar has gone silent and soon after comes the slow pounding on the door: 'Da-da, Da-da'. Distracted, you finish the fly but dab too much lacquer behind the hook eye. The resultant spillage onto the peacock herl leaves the second Milly Midge sporting a distinct Mohawk. Oh well, variation in nature ...

You begin the search for a third hook that will substitute for a size 12 grub hook, but already your mate's tyres are crunching up the gravel outside — right on 10 a.m. You bundle the two slightly ratty Millys into an already chaotic box and head for the front door. 'Morning!' greets your friend, looking annoyingly neat and organised. 'Great day for it.' He grabs an armful of your gear from the table beside the front door. 'Thought there might be some midges about,' he continues, as you both walk over to his car, 'so I tied up some Millys last night. Here,' he says, reaching for a small film canister on the dash, 'tied up a few for you too.'

TROUT GALLERY

IT'S BEEN A bitter winter's day and my fingers are still thawing as I write. I've just come in from a nearby lake, where I fished in the sort of conditions that cause many anglers to enforce their own closed season even if, technically, there are still places they can fish. The sky was relentlessly grey, oozing a constant drizzle that didn't appear to amount to much, but which ended up soaking any part of me not covered in Gore-Tex. The wind droned at a constant 15 knots, and the temperature never even considered rising above single figures. It was hard fishing, the only redeeming feature being the sense of a small miracle occurring on each of the well-spaced occasions a trout ate my Assassin fly.

However, as if rebelling against the monotone day, the few trout I caught wore carnival costumes. Nearly all the rainbows sported a stripe so red as to seem the work of an over-enthusiastic pre-schooler's paintbrush, not nature. Some wore their stripe against a backdrop of silvery purple. The brown trout were copper with yellow bellies. Many featured dots of luminous red among their black spots.

Uncharacteristically, it was well before sunset when I left the water. By then the cold was seeping beyond my fingertips and the wet tip of my nose and settling deeper. What little activity there had been from the fish seemed to have faded to nothing. On the bleak hillside above, a few early lambs bleated for their mothers. Perhaps it was this sound which reminded me that, while the sheep had to brave the elements and the coming night, I had the option of retreating to sanctuary.

Later, while I sat by the fire watching the steam rise from my gloves, I thought about the colours of trout and how this is something else to admire about these fish, as if there wasn't enough to admire already.

This may be a good time to make the slightly contradictory disclosure that I'm actually mildly colour-blind — I have trouble distinguishing between pastel shades of certain colours. I discovered this handicap, appropriately, in the local tackle shop when I was eleven years old. I was spending some hard-earned pocket money on Celta lures, and I asked the proprietor for two of the red, green and silver ones behind the counter. 'Ah, you mean the red and silver ones?' he replied.

'No,' I insisted, pointing determinedly at the red, green and silver models over his shoulder (was he blind?). 'Those ones.' After a few more minutes of mutual exasperation, I gave a frustrated sigh. 'Look, I'll get them myself,' I announced, walking behind the counter. The proprietor gave what I imagined to be a self-chastising shake of his head and took my money.

However, the seed of doubt had been planted and later at home Mum confirmed that the green I saw on Celta blades was actually dull red. Subsequent tests confirmed I had some colour-blindness, putting paid to a career as either a fighter pilot or electrician, but quite possibly enhancing my ability to spot camouflaged animals, including trout: the degree of colour confusion I experience, on which effective camouflage relies, is lessened.

But even with the less-than-perfect rods and cones in my eyes, the vibrancy and range of colouration across the salmonids I have caught is breathtaking. Little wonder that among anglers at least, the common names for locally distinct trout are nearly as numerous as the rivers themselves.

Some scientists aren't so convinced, grouping trout and salmon into disappointingly few species. Within, say, the species *Salmo trutta* (brown trout) all the variations we see in size, colour and even physical appearance are basically regarded as just that — variations. Apparently the tiny cave trout of Italy (it matures at just 5 inches), the virtually spot-free trout of North Africa and the trophy browns of New Zealand could all interbreed and produce fertile offspring.

It is true that trout are so capable of making physical adaptations to a given environment that a batch of brother and sister trout could be rendered unrecognisable from each other simply by varying the environment they grow up in. A fish raised in a cold, acidic and tannin-stained upland creek might be no more than 10 inches long in old age. But by the same time its sea-run sibling, plundering the clear-water bounty of estuary and ocean, could have become a silver 20-pounder.

As my hands dried and the fire glowed on my face, I began to recall the different species (or at least variations) of trout I have caught, and in an idle game with myself I tried to rate them.

First, the chars. These came to mind, appropriately, as the salmonids tolerant of the coldest water. The range of char extends almost to the North Pole, and they have been observed feeding in sub-zero salt water. Of the many distinct species of char, I've caught three: brook trout (*Salvelinus fontinalis*), Arctic char (*S. alpinus)* and white-spotted char (*S. leucomaenis*). For an Australian, char are perhaps the most exotic of salmonids — our rivers and lakes are mostly too warm for them. The only char found here are brook trout, and then in very few waters.

Despite their limited distribution I've caught plenty of brook trout in the Snowy Mountains and Tasmania — if you find them and they're feeding, brookies are not hard to fool. However, it was a brook trout I caught in the Yu River in Japan that I recall more vividly than any other. Perhaps it was as much the circumstances under which it was caught as the fish itself that made it so.

Earlier, I'd fished a stretch of this small, snaggy stream in northern Honshu that was so crowded with flyfishers it defied belief. But after walking some distance upriver, I reached a section that was deserted. I never quite worked out why this was so. Could it be that this part of the Yu was supposed to offer inferior fishing? Was it the fear of bear attack? Signs warned of this, although we'd established earlier that the actual risk was very low. Or was it simply the case that the typical Japanese angler enjoyed the quiet camaraderie of fishing near others?

In any case, when I cut across a bend and briefly left my fishing companion Jamie behind, there was not a soul in sight. It occurred to me later that this was the only time during my visit to Japan that there was no sign of humanity. Deciduous forest lapped the slopes of the

2500-metre-high, cloud-topped mass of Nantai-san volcano, spreading to the river in front of me and the high ranges beyond. Within the amphitheatre of national park there were no visible buildings or road scars.

Ironically, the brook trout appeared to be slightly less abundant than through the heavily fished section downstream, but it didn't take me long to locate a rise. This trout was feeding towards the top-left side of a long, sandy run, clipping down caddis as they fluttered beneath the heavy bows of a cherry blossom tree in flower. As I snuck closer, I could easily make out the shape of the fish as it glided back and forth, selecting only the caddis that actually stayed on the water. I'd learned earlier that the Yu brookies were understandably line shy, so I crawled into position just upstream of the fish and well back from the bank. Although the Shaving Brush I'd fished all morning wasn't a perfect copy of the caddis, I left it on, unwilling to remove a pattern that had succeeded earlier.

The first cast looked good, the fly landing just above the fish and slightly to my side of it. I mended gently to maintain a realistic drift; the trout acknowledged the fly with a slight deviation, then ignored it. The next cast landed a little further upstream and I made a bolder mend, simultaneously snaking slack line through the rod tip. The brookie came over to the Shaving Brush, looked at it for a moment, and then sipped it down.

The fish was 12 inches long — above average for the Yu, but no monster. What struck me about it was the contrast between its reddish-brown body and the way its creamy white spots almost glowed in the hazy light. I caught many other brookies that day, but it's the one beneath the pink blossom I remember best.

Many Japanese streams also carry white-spotted char. They are native to Japan and locally known as *iwana*. *Iwana* appear to be an abundant and successful fish, and I observed wild populations in several mountain fastwaters. I admired the *iwana* I caught for their alertness (whole schools would vanish in an instant if you so much as landed a cast too heavily), and their ability to thrive without artificial intervention in one of the most densely populated countries on earth. *Iwana* are pretty enough too, with their white spots transforming to reddish-orange above the lateral line.

However, I think my favourite char is the Arctic char. The name alone carries a certain majesty befitting the world's northernmost freshwater fish. Most Arctic char populations are found around (or not too far south of) the Arctic Circle, but some relic populations exist in uplands further south still. These are the descendants of Arctic char that were stranded, if you like, they retreated to the cold water of the mountains when the last Ice Age faded.

My encounters with Arctic char have so far been limited to the Alm River and its tributaries in the Austrian Alps. Although the Arctic char is native to the Alm, its numbers, along with those of brown trout and introduced rainbows and brookies, are supplemented by stocking. Following a wonderful flyfishing session on the Alm with my de facto guide and local fishing club member Johann, he took me on a tour of his 'hatchery'. It was little more than an ice-cold spring creek with sections fenced off to house growing trout of different sizes and species. By hatchery standards the fish numbers were relatively low, and Johann said he didn't even need to feed them every day, such was the natural productivity of the creek. I imagined that any fish released into the river, not 200 metres away, would have little difficulty making the transition.

Johann carried a grayling he'd caught for dinner earlier on the Alm, and when we reached a large pool on a bend in the spring creek, he knelt in the grass and cleaned the fish. Casually he passed me the guts. 'There,' he said in good English, pointing to a low wooden jetty which extended into the pool, 'dangle them over the end, and feed the fish — don't let the guts touch the surface.'

Intrigued, I did as instructed. Although the creek was very clear, the bottom was carpeted in dark weed and the sky was overcast, so I couldn't see anything beneath the water. I dangled the guts as instructed. Nothing happened, and then just as I was about to ask for further advice, a 20-inch Arctic char shot from the pool and took all the guts and very nearly my fingertips before the pull of gravity drew it (reluctantly, I imagined) back into the dark pool. I was speechless and Johann laughed out loud. But when I'd recovered from the surprise, I was left with a lasting picture of a hooked-jawed, toothy fish with bright white and orange spots against flanks of almost iridescent blue.

With a common name like 'brown trout', *Salmo trutta* is off to an unpromising start in the trout glamour stakes. However, as any regular angler knows, browns can be anything but, well, brown. Fishing from a sunny Danish beach, I landed a little Baltic sea-run brown that was silver and aqua blue, with no brown on it at all. In Austria I caught brown trout that were admittedly brown, yet with bellies so butter-yellow it seemed the colour might stain my fingers.

It's difficult to think of a favourite rainbow trout (they're all beautiful, even the chrome maidens). However, there is no contest when it comes to the winning member of the rainbow's genus, *Oncorhynchus*. It is undoubtedly the cherry salmon, or *yamame*, which I caught in the Daiya River in Japan. In his magnificent book *Trout of the World*, James Prosek describes the parr marks of *yamame* as plum-coloured, set against a pink that resembles the colour of cherry blossom.

Where I fished it, the Daiya had already rushed down its wide, bouldery bed from the high mountains, leaving the late cherry blossom blooms behind. So, as a number of *yamame* to a pound or so clipped down my brown parachute dun from among a pleasing hatch of naturals, I was unable to hold one up to a nearby blossom-covered slope to compare it. But at any rate, I trust Prosek's description (he is a gifted artist) enough to offer it here. And as I sit here now, a world away in an Australian winter, I have no doubt the *yamame is* the most beautiful of all the salmonids in the gallery of my mind.

ROD AND LINE

ALTHOUGH FLYFISHING SELDOM ceases completely over winter (except perhaps in Alaska), it is certainly the best time of year to spend a few hours sorting out gear.

This is in contrast to when the season is in full swing, when the most many of us can manage is to keep our equipment one or two steps ahead of chaos. Fly boxes become progressively disorganised, leaders are replaced less frequently than they should be, small wader leaks go unrepaired, and the last of a crucial breaking strain of tippet is continually being pulled from a near-empty spool. Fly-line cleaning (or lack of it) becomes a source of quiet shame.

As for fly stocks, mine inevitably shrink in direct proportion to time on the water. Some of my fishing friends bring their tying kits with them on our trips, and replace the required flies around the campfire with cheerful efficiency. However, my own fly-tying skills fall on the wrong side of adequate, and the best I can usually manage is to tie the bare minimum of an important pattern the night before departure (see the earlier chapter, 'Fiddler on the Vise'). I'm fortunate to have a couple of mates who are gifted professional fly tiers, but as one recently pointed out when I asked for 'two dozen Royal Wulffs by the following day please', he's a fly tier, not a conjurer.

So winter is the season to make amends, to stock up on the obvious patterns at least. These will be reliably signposted by one or two ratty survivors lingering in near-empty rows (it's surprising how grimly you'll hang on to an effective fly when there aren't any left to take its place). Inspired by the newly purchased and/or tied replacements, you can then return the fly boxes to something like order.

Winter is also a good opportunity to replenish those other consumables you've run out of (or are about to) like leaders, tippet and floatant. Time is on your side in winter, and a trip to the fly shop can be an enjoyable experience. This is in contrast to mid-season purchases, usually preceded by a comment en route to the fishing destination like, 'Oh bugger! I don't think I've got any 2-kilogram tippet left,' and resulting in a rushed rummage through a dusty corner in an ominously generic small town 'Sports Store' for gear (if you can find it at all) that is either overpriced or out of date.

Yes, a trip to the fly shop on a wintry Saturday morning is a much more fulfilling exercise. For a start, you choose exactly where you spend your money. You know the staff, the range is good, and best of all there is no rush — in fact, the way that rain's coming down outside, the longer it takes the better. If you're feeling really organised, you might even prepare a list beforehand. It might not fit the vagabond trout-bum image to be crossing things off a piece of paper as you go, but it beats discovering you've forgotten something essential when you're hundreds of miles from anywhere in a few months time.

Winter is also a sensible time to contemplate more substantial purchases. Perhaps you began to notice late last season that your rod of several years was no longer state of the art, or that the rattle in the reel was getting worse. Fly vests are not immortal either, and there comes a time when loyalty to Old Faithful must be weighed against the fact that every re-stitched pocket is quickly followed by a new tear.

Thinking especially of new rods, the more considered the purchase, the better. A few chapters back I mentioned my first fly rod, a 9-foot 7-weight fibreglass monstrosity that cast like a length of heavy plastic hose. More than three decades on, I still struggle to use that rod, and it is sobering to reflect that it might easily have put me off flyfishing forever.

The good news is that fly rods that bad are almost unknown today. There is perhaps no area of flyfishing to which technology has been kinder, the only drawback being the vast and confusing range of rods on offer. Even a modestly stocked fly shop is likely to contain a bewildering range of options, so it pays to have a rough idea what you want, what you need and what you should expect before you walk through the door. You're unlikely to encounter anything as crippling as my first rod, but the wrong rod will still prove a handicap. So, for those still grappling with the subject of rod selection, I hope I can help here.

Every fly rod has two fundamental features that determine what type of fishing it is best suited to: the load under which it flexes most effectively, and its length. The first feature is generally referred to, somewhat confusingly, as the rod's weight. It has nothing to do with how much the rod weighs on a set of scales, but rather the weight of line the rod throws best. It is impossible to discuss this rod feature without talking a little bit about line weight first, so let me explain.

To go back a step, in many respects it is the fly *line* more than the fly *rod* that distinguishes flyfishing from all other forms of angling. Uniquely, the fly line is effectively the projectile the flyfisher casts, whereas in every other form of fishing, the terminal tackle — be that a sinker, float, weighted lure or a combination of these — is the projectile the angler casts. In these other forms of fishing, the line exists only to connect the angler to the hook and (hopefully!) the fish.

As the fly line itself is the projectile propelled, flyfishing has unique advantages. The capacity to cast the tiniest, lightest, most buoyant fly great distances is just one of these. And by the way, the fly-line advantage is worth remembering next time someone tells you flyfishing is nothing but a deliberately complicated way of catching fish. Flyfishing may be challenging to master but, because of the capabilities offered by the fly line, at times it will out-fish any other method.

Anyway, back to fly-line weight, and to simplify a little, every fly line (regardless of whether it is designed to float or sink) is constructed to weigh the right amount to perfectly load a certain 'weight' of fly rod. Unless you are flyfishing at the extreme end, the line weights likely to be encountered range from 0 weight (very light) through to 12 weight (very heavy). For most trout fishers, the likely range narrows further from about 2 weight to 7 weight, and this in turn becomes the range of rod weight classes usually considered.

Outfits at the lighter end do one thing very well: they land fly, leader and particularly line on the water delicately. From a hunter–

gatherer point of view, this is the solitary advantage of the lightweights, albeit a substantial one. On some days, on some waters, being able to land fly and line on the water as gently as possible can be the difference between success and failure.

In any event, few of us flyfish just for food, and many anglers choose light rods more for reasons relating to their broader enjoyment of the sport — for example, matching a small creek with a rod that bends easily under the weight of a diminutive trout. It may not be easy to measure the fish-catching advantage using a 2-weight rod versus a 6-weight on a tiny brook, but the aesthetics are obvious. Incidentally, some flyfishers insist that light rods are also less tiring to cast than heavier ones. I'd agree this is an issue at the heavy end of saltwater rods, but if you find a trout rod of any weight tiring to cast, might I gently suggest you're not doing enough fishing?

Heavier rod–line combinations can cast further (up to a point), cast better in wind, and can, if need be, cast heavier flies. And notwithstanding some arguments to the contrary, I'm convinced heavier outfits are better suited to fighting and landing large fish.

Now to length, being the second fundamental feature of fly rods. (Incidentally, there is no necessary relationship between rod weight and rod length, despite a tendency for very light rods to be short). Short rods can only boast two advantages: portability and the ability to operate in tight places. However, on locations like small overgrown streams the latter quality is hugely valuable.

Long rods cast further, 'mend' the line better, and for some forms of flyfishing, like loch-style, they're almost essential. Still, 9, 10 or even 11 feet of rod is a lot to carry around, and not just when poking through the undergrowth. Without actually knowing the rod-breakage statistics, I'll bet long rods more often end their days in ceiling fans and slamming doors than short rods.

So, based on the fundamentals of line weight and length alone, the search for the right rod can be narrowed substantially. If you plan to do nothing but fish for trout on windswept lakes, a 10-foot 7-weight rod is likely to be a sensible choice. For exclusive use on small, overgrown brooks, a 6-foot 2-weight rod is a good match. As for an all-rounder, perhaps a 5- or 6-weight rod, 8½ to 9 feet long. Rods 8 weight and over are mainly used in the pursuit of larger saltwater species, or freshwater species bigger than trout.

I should mention here that not even something as defined as a rod's length and weight means it is indisputably the best fit for a given situation. I've known people to successfully target 10-kilogram tuna with 5-weight rods, others to fish tiny creeks with 7-weights (I did this for a while myself when student funds restricted me to a single rod). Fashion, individual skill, preference and budget (not to mention the desire for a particular experience) all skew the answer to what superficially seems a simple question. But then, you've probably already worked out that flyfishing is like that.

There are other choices to make when choosing a fly rod. The material used in construction is one. Rods constructed largely from carbon fibre are by far the biggest sellers these days, and for good reason. They are extremely light and strong, and the better rod makers can tune a rod to perform in a precise way. Pricing is also attractive, with perfectly serviceable carbon-fibre rods retailing for under $200, and even the very best models not much over $1000.

Split-cane fly rods, manufactured by binding tapered strips of bamboo together, have been around for at least 150 years. 'Bamboo' rods are relatively heavy in terms of their physical weight, and the good ones — generally handmade — are expensive. Because of limited production capacity alone, bamboo will never be as popular as carbon fibre. However a couple of highly skilled anglers I know rate their bamboo rods as favourites, so bamboo shouldn't be discounted as an option.

Fibreglass fly rods? Well, after my brutal introduction to fibreglass, I can hardly pretend to give an unbiased appraisal, can I? I will say that the modern ones are probably an improvement on what were available 35 years ago, and some people like them. Then again, some people like fishing for eels.

Moving on to rod action — yet another ambiguous and mysterious flyfishing term, guaranteed to leave the average novice looking like they've seen a Martian. But fear not; in this context, 'action' basically means where along a rod's length it curves when loaded up. Slow action rods bend along most of their length, fast action rods bend mainly at the tip, and medium action rods bend somewhere in between.

Even within a particular material, length or weight range, different rods can have a different action. I won't begin to predict which action a given angler will prefer, and the best way of determining this is to cast some rods with varying actions. Once again, winter is the ideal time to wander out the back of the fly shop and try a few rods, or even head down to the local casting pool with some mates and your combined rod collections. You can cast away with no distractions from rising fish.

Next, you should consider how many pieces your rod should break down to. This is a more important factor than you might think. Unless you are lucky enough to live right on the water, where you can simply grab your assembled rod off the verandah pegs every time you fancy a fish, you will need to transport your rod. I haven't bought a two-piece rod for more than a decade, having decided that, as a minimum, my rod needs to fit *inside* my aircraft luggage. Most four-piece models do this comfortably, thereby avoiding the possibility of a lonely rod tube rolling into some dark crevice inside an aircraft's baggage hold. Four-piece rods are also more convenient to pack for a long car trip and even to store at home. Many fly rods are now available in four pieces, and there is no performance penalty. Just remember to check that all three joins are tight when the rod is assembled, and then check them again from time to time while actually fishing.

Four-piece rods are okay for backpacking, but the ideal is a six-piece. Six-piece models are much rarer than four pieces, however they fold down into a tube that seems sinfully short. You almost want to carry a six-piece around in your briefcase just because you can.

By the way, avoid three-piece and five-piece rods — they can't be folded neatly in half for short car trips or walks through the bush. If that seems like a petty concern, try putting up with it for a few years and see what you think then.

It would be remiss of me not to mention a host of other little things that could be listed under the heading 'rod finish' — guide numbers, type and spacing, binding quality, colour, gloss or matt finish, reel mount, handle material and so on. I can't really claim to have ever chosen (or declined) a rod based on any of these features, which in one sense could suggest they're not important. On the other hand, I've never had to put up with a rod with, say, worn guides or a loose reel seat, which certainly would be a problem.

As for rod colour and matt or gloss, this has been a source of cheerful debate since Izaak Walton was a boy. There is no disputing that a drab-coloured rod with as little glint or shine as possible is the most practical — the fewer things to alert the fish that someone up to no good is lurking nearby, the better. However, rod manufacturers counter that it isn't easy asking customers to part with several hundred dollars for something that looks like it's been rolled in the mud.

Finally, there's the question of warranty. Fly-rod warranties vary from almost embarrassingly generous, as in break the rod over your knee in the shop and get a new one, to non-existent. With the more expensive rods, an impressive-sounding warranty is often a significant factor in the decision to buy, so it is worth researching exactly what it means in practice. The experiences of other owners of that brand, and the advice of a reputable fly shop, are the best way to establish what really happens if you break your new baby. While most people are happy (even pleasantly surprised) with warranty service, among those who are not, the *time* taken to repair or replace a broken rod is the most common cause of grief. One of my clients was still waiting on a replacement tip six months after he made his claim, which obviously defeats the point.

Most rod stories have happier endings. There's something about the first outing with a new rod, particularly one you've taken some time choosing. For once, it really is true that catching a fish is a bonus, because simply casting and fishing the rod is pleasure enough. Not that you'll decline the opportunity of a fish if it's offered — and in the counter-intuitive way of flyfishing, the fact that you aren't desperate for a trout means that you catch one. So, the rod works. Then you catch another, and although you're not superstitious, the thought crosses your mind that maybe, just maybe, this is a lucky rod ...

THE GULF

WHEN I ARRIVED in Australia's far north in June, it was, strictly speaking, winter: even in the tropics there was marginally less daylight than in summer, and it was a few degrees cooler. Yet the conditions bore little resemblance to the winter I'd left down south. Each day when I rose before sunrise from my bunk aboard the Carpentaria Seafaris' mothership, *Tropic Paradise*, it was always to pleasant, enveloping warmth. Back at my southern highland home, winter is a time of semi-hibernation as far as the wildlife is concerned, and dawn the coldest and most silent time of all. Here, however, the air and the water were already thick with life. The tidal current quietly gurgled and hissed against *Tropic Paradise*'s ample hull, the sky turned from faint pink to orange, and seabirds called to each other as their day and ours began. Across the glassy expanse of whichever river mouth we happened to be moored in, fish would invariably be leaping, swirling and bow-waving in the half-light. I never quite got used to the overwhelming sense of wellbeing that came from eating breakfast in a spacious dining area 150 kilometres from civilisation, while watching the fish I'd be spending the next ten hours trying to catch.

The waters of the Gulf of Carpentaria and those that flow into it seem impossibly rich. This warm, shallow sea simply shimmers with untold millions of fish, crustaceans, mammals and reptiles — including crocodiles. At daybreak early in the trip, a 4-metre croc casually crossed from one river bank to the other, coming within 10 metres of a group of us watching from the back of the boat. There was no danger — the guides had told us during our briefing on the way down the coast that you don't have to worry about the crocodiles you can see, within reason! However the ridge-backed log effortlessly waking across the river was a reminder we couldn't be quite as carefree wading or strolling the banks as we were back home.

Overall, the Gulf provides a contrast with those fishing destinations that can hide their inhabitants so well that on a hard day you wonder if anything lives there at all. In the Gulf, nature is on display continuously. It's not always a beautiful display — the endless mangroves clawing at thick grey mud broke the hearts of many an early explorer struggling to reach the open sea after crossing a continent. Even today, the mangrove swamps offer a view only a marine biologist (or barramundi fisher!) could describe as attractive.

Away from the mangroves, whole swathes of dead and broken forest line some riverbanks. At the height of the gentle winter dry season, these skeletal remains seem incongruous, but they remind you of the storm surges and cyclonic winds that must lash the place during the Wet — one of the main reasons permanent human habitation is so limited up here.

Immersed in the predictable, settled weather of the winter dry season, storm-surges and hurricanes seemed as improbable as a fishless day. From the luxurious mobile base of *Tropic Paradise*, I fished hard for more than a week in the company of skipper Greg Bethune, his capable crew, and my ten fellow guests. I'd only met two of my companions before this trip, Joe and Jenny Singe. By the end of it all of us were old friends; anglers bonded by an experience you couldn't quite explain to someone who wasn't there. But I'll try anyway.

Most days the fishing began when we climbed aboard the small powerboats moored at the back of the mothership. There were two, sometimes three anglers plus a guide per boat. The options were pleasantly confusing. You could head up the river and fish the mangrove edges for ambushing predators like barramundi or mangrove jack. You could fish around the sand- and rock-lined lower river for species such as ... well, species too numerous to mention, but trevally and queenfish were always highlights for me. As these stretches were free of the tangled mangroves further upstream, it was often comfortable to cast from the shore, where a wide view and clear water would hopefully provide ample warning of any stalking bities.

At some ill-defined point, yet another option occurred wherever the river mouths merged with the Gulf itself in a mix of endless beaches, expansive flats and a maze of channels. Here perhaps more than anywhere else, the expertise of the guides was paramount as they navigated around treacherous sandbars and dead-end channels, at the same time locating the temporary hotspots that came and went with the ever-changing tides. In these waters giant herring tail-walked after terrified baitfish like scimitars hurled across the water, tarpon threw flies skyward as if playing a game, and the ubiquitous queenfish pursued everything, including our flies, with zealous determination. And maybe, just maybe there would be a chrome underwater flash of a 'mooning' permit or the dark sickle tail of one breaking the surface.

One morning the fishing on the river mouth flats was especially memorable, and that evening I lay in my bunk and wrote it up in my journal while the tarpon splashed in the floodlight beams outside. The story later appeared in *Flyfisher* magazine as part of a larger feature.

Joe, Jenny and I spent the morning pursuing permit with expat Canadian guide Al Simson. With the tide ebbing steadily, Al manoeuvred the boat towards a particular inshore flat which was sheltered by two slowly emerging sandbars. Only a couple of minutes after entering the flat, Al spotted a dark mass 150 metres away and immediately suspected permit. We could see the distant shadow the moment he pointed it out, but how Al guessed it wasn't just a school of any old species, I'll never know. As we moved closer, tell-tale 'mooning' confirmed Al's call.

Schooling permit are said to be easier to catch than ones and twos, but as Joe and I frantically changed Clousers for crab patterns, 'easy' was not a term that sprung to mind. Almost inert presentations are required when fishing crab flies to permit. As Al snuck the boat to within casting range, I struggled to reconcile the drifting boat, moving school and a stiff headwind with an inert presentation using an intermediate line. 'Oh, and you need to keep in contact with the fly,' said Al. 'They'll pick it up and spit it out pretty quick.'

As the permit moved busily along the bottom, I landed a few casts among them, but for no result. I became more and more concerned I was getting takes, but failing to detect them because I wasn't managing the line correctly. Meanwhile Joe was doing better with two good takes on a brown crab pattern, although the hook failed to hold. With my confidence in both my presentation and fly crumbling, Al threw me a lifeline. 'Try a Gotcha,' he suggested. 'You can give it a few twitches like a shrimp.'

I made the fastest fly change in history, but by the time I was ready to cast, the permit were looking nervous. They appeared to be more interested in fleeing the boat than feeding. Had we missed our chance? Al repositioned the boat a final time to intercept the school. They were moving quickly as they came past the bow about 20 metres away. Although our odds had diminished with every failed ambush of the permit, I felt a burst of confidence casting a new fly, especially one I could actually move to keep in contact with. The presentation looked good, I waited for the fly to sink, stripped a little and I was on.

The permit didn't scream off as Al expected. Instead it took line steadily and relentlessly. For the next half hour it was almost as if the fish was pacing itself, allowing small gains in line, only to pull more off against a drag so tight it made the line sing and hum in the wind. Eventually the boat drifted onto the downwind sandbank, allowing me to jump out and resume the tussle from land. Although this raised the danger of the permit making it to the channel at the end of the sandbank and into open sea, I was relieved to have the freedom to walk around unhindered. It was also a relief not to be faced with landing the fish from the boat — something I always dread with large fish.

The 40-minute mark of the contest approached and, for just a moment, the fish relented and briefly I levered it into the shallows. It charged back out again instantly, but it was the encouragement I needed. When I applied more side strain, the permit darted back and forth less confidently, no longer able to swim fully upright in the shallow water. Finally I seized my chance, pulled it off balance and walked it up on to the sand while Al backed up with the net. An 18-pound permit lay quietly on its side, and the ghosts of all my big fish losses in recent times blew away on the tropical breeze.

The sandy beaches outside the river mouths were another place you could fish from the shore if you chose, and I really enjoyed wandering these on my own for an hour or two. It was always surprising how quickly my 'ride' would vanish into the vastness once I was dropped off, leaving me on the empty beach like the last man on earth.

Offshore we hunted pelagics like tuna and mackerel. The tuna usually travelled in schools, and on a relatively calm morning (which was typical) you could see them churning the deep-blue water from a kilometre away. The prized longtail, or northern bluefin, tuna created dots of white on the distant surface as they leapt after fleeing baitfish. Meanwhile the mackerel tuna could turn a whole acre of water to foam as they surged after their prey. The mack tuna were sometimes so tightly packed it looked as if you could literally have walked across them. When they boiled in unison, they sounded like a heavy rapid on a trout stream.

Besides the tuna, the guides looked for bait balls. These are compressed schools of little fish, distinguishable as dark sub-surface shapes somewhere between the size of a car and a house, driven together by an extreme (and sometimes ultimately deluded) sense of safety in numbers. You never knew what might be lurking around a bait ball — Spanish mackerel, cobia or billfish, as well as super-sized versions of other species like golden trevally and queenfish. One time as we approached a ball, the guide saw a marlin and told me to change my 9-weight rod for a borrowed 12-weight. I cast a blue and white fly the size of my hand into the edge of the ball, heart racing, half hoping a marlin would hit it, half hoping it wouldn't. There was a crashing take and the line screamed from the reel, but it was 'only' a 15-pound longtail.

So the days went past. Among our group there were fishing adventures of almost every kind imaginable to be retold over a cold drink and a platter of longtail sashimi each night on the warm deck. Huge fish landed or bitten in half by sharks, lines broken (and even rods!), rare species, or sights no one would believe — except we did, because we were there.

One day I was fishing a remote river mouth. Where I fished, the powerful tidal currents cut hard into the sand between two bars of rotten rock, perhaps 100 metres apart. The firm sand dropped steeply into the slightly tannin-stained flow that swirled past.

The drop-off and foam-streaked eddies provided an ideal fishing spot, except only half my effort was directed at fooling a fish with the fly; the other half was alert for crocodiles. I was only game to fish on foot at all because the steep bank and clearish water offered a good lookout for any approaching beasties.

After a while I hooked and eventually landed a nice golden trevally. I was just beaching it when in my peripheral vision I glimpsed a huge dark shape launch itself from the river and up onto the bank, not 50 metres from where I stood. By the time I'd snapped my head around for a better look, the creature was disappearing back into the water.

I quickly released the trevally and strode a few metres further back from the water's edge, more curious than scared by what I'd just seen. I was certain it wasn't a croc — I'd sighted a few of those in recent days and they were scaly and unmistakably ridged, not as dark and smooth as whatever it was that had just rocketed from the river. Instead I was thinking maybe a pilot whale (do they have them up here?), even a very dark dolphin. There was also a chance that what I'd seen was a large shark, and this possibility kept me walking well away from the water while I polaroided the edge seeking an answer to the mystery.

I didn't have to wait long before I saw something again. At first I thought it was a patch of reef or weed, but it was actually moving along the light sand on the very edge of the river. It was a stingray — the biggest I've ever seen, perhaps 2 metres across the wings. I stepped slowly down the bank to get a closer look as it came past.

The giant ray was gliding unhurriedly towards me and about ten paces to my left when a small crab scurried out of the water between us and stopped about an arm's length up the beach. I swear it brushed its forehead with a claw, crab speak for 'Phew, that was close.' The ray stopped alongside the crab, barely submerged. Then in a blur of movement incongruous for such a massive creature it flew from the water, spread its huge wings over the sand like a cape, and then slid gracefully back into the river. The whole process took perhaps three seconds and at the end of it there was no sign of the crab.

Transfixed, I watched as the ray continued its silent patrol. It paused right in front of me, so close I could have touched it with my foot. Its strange cat-like eyes stared at me long and hard, and I had a powerful sense of something like intelligence. I can't explain why, but there seemed to be great age in those eyes, as if the stingray had been patrolling this wilderness river forever.

The ray moved effortlessly along to the right and continued its hunt. I began to fish again half-heartedly, but I was too distracted, so I gave up and just sat on the sand and watched. There turned out to be two rays, the second one just as big as the first. They shared the beat between the rock bars and never seemed to get in each other's way. Periodically another crab would scurry out from the water, but never far enough. Without fail, the crabs disappeared beneath the giant black wings, never to be seen again. Unlike the rays, the crabs wouldn't (or couldn't) learn.

Eventually some imperceptible change took place on the river. Maybe it was the turn of the tide or maybe there were no more crabs. Whatever, the rays abruptly vanished into the depths, and only a series of 2-metre-wide scrapes in the sand proved I hadn't dreamt the whole thing.

SPRING

A Stream for September

In my home state of Victoria, the beginning of spring coincides rather neatly with the opening of the stream trout season, which falls on the first Saturday in September. You might imagine, even expect, that I would celebrate both events appropriately by going stream fishing. Alas, I'm yet to actually manage this, something of which at least a few of my fishing mates take a dim view. I plead competition from some very good lake fishing locally (September is a prime month), and the fact that inviting stream conditions can be hard to find during this generally cool, wet and windy time of year.

But one day in the third week of last September, a rare combination beckoned. The sun was out, the breeze had temporarily eased to a gentle zephyr, and a few successive days of no rain suggested the local streams would be running at fishable height and clear. Most importantly I had a few free hours — a feature not infinitely available to fishing writers, despite what you might hear.

I ran through a quick checklist of possible candidates for a visit. I wanted somewhere that had maintained at least some water (and therefore trout) through a dry summer, and which was also close enough for an afternoon trip. In the end I decided on a stream I'd last checked in the dying days of autumn. On that occasion I'd spotted three fish in a 100-metre stroll without the rod, so that in itself was a reason to go back.

After a few months away, you never quite know what you'll find when returning to a stream that may have experienced all sorts of events — good and bad — in your absence. I pulled off down the laneway that ran to a little reserve beside the road bridge. It was late morning and the spring sun shone warmly though the windscreen, but when I opened the door I was surprised by the bite in the air, and any thought of shorts and boots fishing was sensibly forgotten for a pair of waders. I'd intended to rig up the rod before I peered over the bank — if a fish is spotted immediately on the season's first stream trip, this can lead to all sorts of subsequent confusion and forgotten gear. However, as soon as I'd pulled on the waders I broke this rule and sneaked a peek.

The stream was flowing well, with only a slight tinge of colour — around 4 metres wide in the runs and riffles, spreading to perhaps twice that width in the pools. The shadows of the surrounding gums, willows and wattles inhibited the view beneath the surface and I didn't immediately sight a trout, which meant I could return to setting up in an orderly fashion.

Eventually I was ready to fish. At first the closed canopy around the stream felt a little claustrophobic after many months on open lakes, but gradually I got used to short casts and the imposed finesse smaller rivers demand. Well, almost. There were still some moments when the fly found branches instead of water, and I spooked one good fish from a pocket I should have noticed before I was about to step in it.

By the time the noon sun passed overhead, I'd seen a couple more trout but my fly, a parachute Royal Wulff, had gone untouched. Perhaps I was being ambitious hoping for dry-fly fishing when it was more the end of winter than the beginning of spring, so I tied a small bead-head nymph to a dropper beneath the dry.

The stream and its trout continued to be cryptic. Although these western Victorian creeks can resemble eastern fastwaters, especially during the bountiful flows of spring, the fish (almost all browns) tend to be fewer, larger and less predictable. The trout will hold in the better runs and pockets, but just as often they'll cruise the fertile weedbeds and edges — you can be carefully fishing upstream, only to notice a fish swimming right towards you at the last moment, with predictable consequences.

I'd spooked a couple of trout this way before I arrived at a tight bend. There was a break in the trees so I stopped and made the most of the direct sunlight to scan the water. Nothing showed, and then, just as I was about to cast anyway, I glimpsed the tail of a trout waving as it cruised slowly upstream over the submerged weed on the far bank. It was only a glimpse but it was unmistakeable. In moments the trout had disappeared beneath the weed and I searched in the direction it was headed, hoping for another clue. Beneath a willow branch upstream I thought I saw a faint swirl and presented the flies. They began to drift back towards me untouched, but then I saw a flicker behind them and a good trout appeared in hot pursuit. Hoping to encourage it to do something reckless, I twitched the Wulff ... and the fly sank! Not deterred, the trout shot past the nymph and engulfed the drowned dry as if it had been looking for it all day.

The strike was hardly necessary, and by the time I lifted the rod, the fish was already dancing all over the pool, then diving for the weed. The whole situation had caught me slightly by surprise, leaving me feeling as if I was very much the follower, not the one in control. But everything held together and soon I was beaching the trout in the wet backside grass; a fat, silvery 2-pounder that looked more like a lake trout than one from a shady stream. At any rate, the stream season had begun on a high note and the only question was whether I could legitimately claim the maiden fish as caught on the dry?

I cast my mind back twelve months to the previous year's opening and reflected that it didn't really matter — a trout caught, on wet or dry, was reason enough to celebrate. On that occasion, it was again two or three weeks into the season when Peter Julian and I eventually found a matching free day and headed out for a few hours on another nearby stream to christen the new season.

By good luck we struck a bluebird morning, and there was only the faintest hint of early spring sharpness in the air as we climbed down a steep bank to the water. The creek was near perfect fishing level. To find a comfortable flow during what should have been the wettest time of year was a concern for the summer months ahead. But ever the pragmatist, Peter ventured, 'Well, it's ideal *now*.' He peered appreciatively downstream, and then added, 'Hey, I think I saw a rise.' Peter was already making his way through the long grass and tea-tree when he suggested, 'I'll poke down and investigate, if you want to fish up from here.'

That arrangement was fine by me, because just then I thought I saw a disturbance in the little pool immediately upstream. It was no more than a gentle ripple coming out from the near bank, towards the top of the pool. I'd already tied on a size 14 Parachute Adams, gambling that the low water and mild day might produce not only the first stream trout of the season, but also the first on the dry.

With a couple of metres of line drawn and the fly in my fingertips, I stepped carefully towards the tail of the pool. Stealth or not, the 14-inch brown I nearly trod on wasn't impressed. I was, however, alert enough to notice its bow-wave being joined by a second as it headed towards the run at the top. Trout A, Weigall E+ (a fail, but at least I noticed the trout at the head of the pool).

Chastened, I approached the next pool as if it were guarded by sleeping Dobermans. This was a nice piece of water. It was only as big as a garden shed, but it was waist deep, and lined on the left side by a network of ancient red-gum roots. This particular spot had produced its share of triumph and tragedy for me over the years, and after my shaky start, I summoned the will to stand well back and watch for a while.

Just when my early season eagerness was ready to override my patience, I saw a rise about a metre out from the roots. 'Aha!' I muttered quietly to myself. I noticed a little bluish dun drifting in the lazy current downstream of the rise, and seconds later it was gone in a swirl. So, perhaps the trout was cruising rather than holding in the current. Sure enough, it rose a third time and I glimpsed the fish as it turned right at the pool tail, before swimming back upstream.

I was pleased my caution had prevented me from blundering straight into the fish as it moved downstream, but there wasn't time to gloat. At the instant when I imagined the trout had reached the top of the pool, I cast quickly to the edge of the red-gum roots, then froze. There were some uneasy moments as the fly began to drift back towards me untouched. Had I cast too short? Then, through a hole in the reflections cast by the old red gum itself, I saw the trout — a 2-pounder at least — bearing down on my fly. I believe it was just opening its mouth to take the Adams when I struck. Unbeknown to me, Peter had caught up a minute or two earlier, just in time to witness the last part of the hunt. Peter has spent much of his working life as a secondary school teacher, and the first I knew of his presence was the sonorous schoolmaster's voice: 'Trout 1, Weigall 0.'

'Actually, Trout 2, Weigall 0,' I replied with uncharacteristic honesty. 'I nearly trod on one in the pool below.'

We fished up the next stretch together. Peter made me feel a bit better by missing one on the strike in the shadows of a large, flat pool — though to be fair, he did appear to lift the rod at the right moment.

Next we came to a narrow pool on a tight bend, fed by an even narrower chute where the water had carved a channel through the bedrock. It was my turn again. I stood back and watched for a minute or two, but nothing moved, so under Peter's watchful gaze from high on the bank I proceeded to carefully search the lower part of the pool.

With painstaking precision, I cast my way slowly upstream, covering every possible lie. Still nothing. Eventually I crawled towards the chute at the top, where surely the pool's resident must be. The chute was only 5 metres long and looked no more than ankle deep. I stared at it until my eyes watered, and then alongside a single protruding rock about halfway up the chute, I noticed the barest disturbance. It was almost indistinguishable from the natural swirls and pulses of current drifting past the rock, but the longer I looked, the surer I was that I hadn't imagined it. 'I reckon there's one right beside that rock,' I murmured.

'Go on then,' said Peter.

An overhanging tea-tree branch obstructed an easy cast, but I somehow managed to flick the Adams under it so it landed about a metre above the rock. The fly drifted nicely with the bubbles, and right on cue a snout stuck out, snipped the Adams off the surface with an audible 'clip', and I lifted. The rod tip bent under the weight of a solid fish ... then sprung back up. Damn! I looked at Peter and shrugged.

'I'm a fair man,' he conceded. 'We'll call that one a draw.'

I stood up to relieve my sore knees, and that's when I instantly spooked two additional trout out of the broken water at the very top of the chute. I looked on forlornly as they shot down past me.

'No doubt about the first day on a small stream,' chuckled Peter, shaking his head as he began walking up to the next stretch. 'It's just like going back to flyfishing school.'

BIG TROUT

IN EARLY SPRING twenty years ago, I was fishing one of my favourite places in Victoria, the southern shore of the Loddon arm of Lake Cairn Curran. Cairn Curran is an unlikely trout lake. Set between harsh granite hills and subject to fierce summer heat, the level of this man-made lake fluctuates enormously depending upon rainfall and demand for irrigation water. However, it can be very productive, and given even a half-decent season, Cairn Curran produces fine fishing for decent brown trout, many of which can be spotted first if you're patient. On this occasion it was September and the lake was rising quite quickly. Unusually, it remained fairly clear, the water more like weak tea than milky coffee.

Around the ruins of a long-abandoned farmhouse, a trout swirled here and there. It was mid morning and the sun beamed down with surprising intensity for so early in spring. Frogs croaked in the flooded grass, and I knelt on a log island which provided just enough elevation that water didn't trickle down the back of my thigh waders. I desperately wanted to cast my fat water-beetle fly, the same one that had fooled several nice trout over the preceding few weeks. But with the flat, bright water, the risk of accidentally scaring the fish with a blind cast was too great. So I waited, the ridges in the log digging into my knees.

It proved wise to be patient for, only minutes later, a trout boiled not two rod lengths in front of me. It required the gentlest side flick of the rod to deliver the water beetle to the right area. I gave the fly a moment to settle, then drew the line slowly through my fingers. There was a swirl a metre to the right, a lunging bow-wave, and I was on. The trout pulled away with frightening force, and I knew immediately that this fish was bigger than the 4- and 5-pounders I had landed recently. But it was several minutes before the fish finally surfaced and I could actually glimpse what I had hooked. A long way out in the lake, I saw a reddish-brown back, the trademark of the biggest Cairn Curran trout, and the distance from dorsal to tail alone seemed as long as my forearm.

Weeks earlier I had lost another monster trout not far from this spot, when the hook simply pulled for no apparent reason. There is surely no more deflating way to lose a big fish, and this time I was shaking with anxiety as I bent the rod into my second chance. Slowly, slowly the fish came towards me. Halfway in, there was an angry run for a clump of submerged thistles, but I was able to turn it at the last moment. Finally the trout was back into the clear corner where I'd first hooked it. It lunged once more for the open water, but the arc of the rod now proved too much for it to fight. I walked steadily backwards now, and at last the big brown was flapping in the flooded grass. It was a humpbacked buck, no doubt an old fish, yet still in its thick-shouldered prime. It weighed 9 pounds, and was my best ever trout from a Victorian public water.

During recent seasons, Cairn Curran has been much lower than during the late 1980s and early 1990s, and the spot where I caught my 9-pounder is today a well-grazed paddock. Just up the road is Cairn Curran's sister lake, Tullaroop, which I talked about in the first chapter. Although it too has suffered the deprivations of drought, enough water has remained to ensure good fishing in recent years.

In this case, it's important to distinguish 'good' fishing from easy or prolific fishing — historically, Tullaroop has rarely been either. However, it's a lake that holds promise at any level, and the trout have always been some of the best in Victoria. So when my friend Mick and I visited Cairn Curran and found the fishing tough, it was an easy decision to make the 15-minute drive to Tullaroop.

We pulled the car up on the north shore of the lake. There was a light parallel breeze and the sunshine was tempered by cirrus cloud. The rising water had only just reached the hardiest weeds but it was even clearer than Cairn Curran. Scarcely had we pulled the rods from the car when a large trout started to absolutely hammer a school of Australian smelt. Crowded nervously against the bank, the smelt had nowhere to go and minnows, bow-waves and spray flew in every direction. Mick was first down, firing short, pinpoint casts into the strike zone. The trout swirled and bumped his fly but didn't connect.

There was scarcely time for Mick to finish cursing when two more fish crashed the smelt further down the bank. We chose one each and ran for them. Mick's kept moving; mine disappeared. About then, I noticed white flashes coming from the shore on the opposite side of the bay to where we were fishing. I was too far away to hear anything, but the more I looked, the more convinced I was that a trout was smelting over there.

I'm not sure why I deserted a promising bank for a distant, uncertain chance, but by the time I had jogged the required 200 metres, I was just in time to see the last crashing attack not a metre from the bank. A smelter indeed! I was too late to cover the fish, but I crept forward, dropped to my knees, and began to pepper the scene of the last charge with a pair of miniature zonker flies. The trout didn't show again but anxious smelt dimpled the water all the way along the bank. I fished the flies back slowly three times, keeping them in the water right up to the edge. Nothing. On the fourth cast, I was just about to lift the flies to re-cast when I felt the faintest pluck. Strange. I cast again, and this time the retrieve came through the same spot undisturbed. Damn. Probably a fish on the previous cast, and probably now spooked. I cast again anyway, and in exactly the same spot I felt a gentle pluck once again. This time I lifted into solid resistance.

One head shake and I knew it was a trout, a second massive wrench and I knew, without seeing anything, that I'd hooked a monster. Then the fish took off — steadily at first, and then faster and faster. I yelled out to Mick. This was a trout that, even if ultimately lost, I wanted to share with someone. Mick, bless him, deserted the smelter he was casting to and came running around the bay. 'Look, another beauty out behind yours!' shouted Mick as he ran.

'That's the one on my line!' I replied. I could no longer see my fly line, just backing disappearing into the water only roughly in the direction of the dorsal and tail now cutting across the surface an alarming distance offshore.

Somehow, turn by turn, I worked line back onto reel. The brutal headshakes continued though, each one threatening to break something vital. I've only ever had one backing knot fail (don't ask) but it was a huge relief to get the first bit of plastic-coated line back on the spool. Eventually the trout was close to the gently sloping bank. I more-or-less beached it, with Mick backing up on the net. The fish was a wild female brown trout, very well recovered from spawning. Mick generously guessed it was a 10-pounder (I didn't dare), but the weigh net confirmed it at a fraction over 9 pounds, or 4 kilograms. When I went to let the fish go, I pulled the fly from its jaw only to find that it was attached to nothing more than 10 centimetres of loose tippet. Sometime near the very end of the fight, the line had broken.

There are of course many wonderful things about that fish, to the extent that I'm thinking of dividing my life into 'pre-Tullaroop 9-pounder' and 'post-Tullaroop 9-pounder' periods. One of the good things is simply that it was nice to actually land a beauty for a change, after a few other encounters in recent years that haven't gone well. Another plus was brought home to me when a relative newcomer to the fly asked me when I'd landed my biggest Victorian trout. 'Just a couple of years ago,' I replied. And no disrespect to that marvellous Cairn Curran fish from two decades back, but it sounded a lot better than saying '1989'.

CHANGE OF PLAN

THERE ARE FEW things in life that bring a deeper sense of contentment than the moment when a fishing trip is locked in. You hang up the phone or log off the computer, sit back for a few moments, and let the idea sink in. The flights and cabin are booked, and the trip is no longer something abstract that *might* happen, it's a reality.

If the trip is to somewhere new, then part of the anticipation is not knowing exactly what to expect. You'll read what you can beforehand of course, pore over maps and quiz anyone you can think of who might have some information, but until you step out of the car or off the plane, your destination is a mystery.

Trips to familiar locations are no less enticing, only in these cases you look forward to revisiting things and places which (we can assume) you've already formed a distinct liking for. You've been to some spots often enough that, as soon as the trip is organised, you're already imagining the details. There's that pool about 300 metres below the bridge which arcs toward the west, and you can already picture yourself fishing from the east bank around sunset and watching big trout sipping just off the boulders on the far side.

You might even daydream about something not directly related to the fishing, like walking across the paddock to the river with the grass still wet with dew and mist over the backwaters. Perhaps it's an after-dinner drink on the verandah that comes to mind, with the stream murmuring somewhere in the dark below and frogs chirruping to the stars.

Now, in some corner of your intellect, you know that no location, especially no high-latitude trout-fishing destination, is going to repeatedly offer the same conditions every time you visit. But experience is an all-powerful influence on imagination. You just know that, hundreds of kilometres away, those sippers by the boulders are waiting for you as reliably as a scene from a favourite movie.

A couple of years ago I had a late spring trip to New Zealand where the favourite movie was, metaphorically speaking, rewritten, edited and then had a few significant characters replaced for good measure. With father-and-son companions Ian and James, I headed to the central South Island of New Zealand, arriving on the tail of one of the wettest Novembers on record. After several previous visits to the area, the three of us were quietly confident we knew what to expect. We were loosely aware there had been a bit of rain, but we had dealt with wet weather before. And not to appear smug about it, but we had also refined our itinerary to the point where it posed an almost ruthless threat to the local trout. We knew where to fish, we knew how, and we knew when.

The first sign that things mightn't quite go to plan came when I called a mate who guides in the area. I eagerly sought confirmation about the status of one of the rivers we were most looking forward to. Would it be better to wait until later in the trip or should we fish it straight away?

'Forget it,' was the blunt response.

'What, for the whole trip?' I asked, and then added lamely, as if it would make any difference, 'But it fished so well last time.'

This brutal advice set the stage for the whole holiday. Rivers we regarded almost as old friends were out, or at least so full of water from late spring rain that previously effective fishing strategies were worthless. At first this was unsettling, to say the least. But slowly we adapted to a familiar fishery turned unfamiliar. Headwater creeks we'd never bothered with were now good-sized streams with, it turned out, good-sized trout — apparently happy to stay up the top of the system while water levels permitted. We also tackled some lowland rivers we'd previously sped across in the car on our way to the 'serious' high-country waters. Put it this way, we won't be speeding over those bridges next trip.

But perhaps the most significant point in the adventure was a visit to one of the rivers that to us (and, given the complete lack of other anglers, everyone else) appeared simply too high to fish. It tore with frightening force between recently collapsed banks and newly gouged channels, icy with glacial silt. Yet driven by something between stubbornness and hope, we were determined to at least cast a line on water that had given so much on previous holidays.

Initially this seemed an empty gesture, with the torrent offering no holding lies for trout and so nowhere worthwhile to cast to. But patient exploration and careful observation gradually revealed exceptions. Some of the turbulent edges actually harboured slower strips of current — often no more than a forearm wide — hidden among the pressure waves and foam. And as we walked further, we came across anabranches where the fury of the main flow was at least dispersed.

For all a trout's remarkable attributes, it's not immune from the laws of physics, and we soon found that the 10 per cent of the river that wasn't flowing at jogging pace or greater held 90 per cent of the fish. So we bypassed lengths of stream that would have occupied us for half a day under regular circumstances, yet spent an hour or more on sections that we'd normally fish in minutes. If anything, the trout were bigger than usual, and once we worked out what to do, we caught at least as many as on previous trips.

'I never thought I'd say this,' said James as the three of us walked back to the car across a field turning orange in the setting sun, 'but I almost prefer this river high.' He paused as he opened an old wire gate, then added, as if he needed to provide an explanation, 'It's more of a challenge really.'

Almost exactly twelve months later, Ian and I were back in the South Island. This time we had planned to fish the West Coast rivers, but two days out a 'Severe Weather Warning for Heavy Rain' on the New Zealand Meteorological Service site had us rapidly redesigning our itinerary. The forecast said in excess of 150 millimetres of rain per day was likely to fall on the West Coast, and we could imagine the clear, bouldery forest streams we knew transformed into terrifying cauldrons, carrying whole trees like dry flies. We changed some bookings and made the central South Island our destination once again.

As we waited for our flight to Christchurch, a last check of the forecast suggested a further deterioration in the weather, with rain now spreading from the west, north and the south. I always travel to New Zealand mentally prepared for bad weather, especially in spring — you can't have that much good trout water without precipitation to feed it — but watching the rainfall maps gradually engulfing the South Island from three directions did leave us feeling a bit under siege.

Our plane landed in Christchurch just before midnight, the runway lights illuminating tarmac glossy with rain. So, it had spread to the east. The wipers on the rental car swished back and forth all the way to our Ashburton motel. Located in the middle of the windswept flatness of the Canterbury Plains, Ashburton isn't a particularly central location for trout fishing, but our room offered the chance for some much needed sleep after a long day and placed us within an easy drive of good water.

The next morning the rain had stopped. I walked out of the motel to the edge of the broad main street and scanned the expansive sky. To the west, a black mass of cloud towered over the Southern Alps; to the north the sky was grey. Immediately south there were streaks of blue sky, but further south still the clouds had a multi-layered look that suggested instability.

With the area unaffected by rain apparently shrinking by the minute, Ian and I changed our plans again. Instead of heading straight for the rivers east of Mount Cook, we decided to try some closer waters. It wasn't so much the idea of fishing in rain that concerned us, but rather its effect on the rivers. While our trip a year earlier had increased our confidence in tackling high flows, there is a limit to what is fishable.

As if to remind us of this fact, a short while later we were driving south and bridging the Rangitata River. This long river rises in the Southern Alps, and the milky torrent several hundred metres wide told of storms that continued to rage in the mountains, belying the patchy sunshine that lit the road ahead of us. The condition of the Rangitata reinforced that we couldn't be too fussy — if we found clear water, we'd be wise to stop and fish it.

At the beautiful town of Geraldine, we left the plains and entered green hills dotted with trees. I never quite get used to how abruptly the New Zealand landscape changes. In minutes we'd departed a plain as flat as a football field that, while attractive in its own big-sky way, bore signs of a constant struggle against drought and wind. Now we wound through paddocks lush with thick grass, contented cattle and copses of bush verging on jungle. We also encountered the first of the hill-country streams. They were too small for serious fishing, but promisingly, they flowed gently and very clear.

Before long we approached a more substantial river, one we'd fished fleetingly on past visits to the South Island. We'd always promised to return for a more serious go, and now circumstances virtually dictated we kept our pledge. Ian located a well-concealed track we'd used before. The track turned off the main road and disappeared into a cluster of dark-green willows, before it emerged on a gravelly floodplain tenuously vegetated by clumps of grass and thistle. I craned my neck to glimpse the river, which was only metres away but concealed by a short, steep bank.

And there it was, mercifully clear and not flowing too strongly. We parked beside a quiet backwater which pulsed gently in response to the rushing river beyond. Given we were virtually encircled by storm systems, the morning air was surprisingly mild and still. Peering over the tops of the tall cottonwoods and poplars fringing the river's floodplain, I could glimpse rain clouds in the middle distance but the sky overhead was only lightly overcast.

Ian and I walked down across the floodplain together, then, where our course bisected the tail of a pleasing pool, we decided to split. Ian started fishing at the pool tail, while I continued downstream a couple more bends.

I've lost count of how many times I've visited New Zealand, but it always takes me a little while to acclimatise during the first session on the water. Partly it's a practice thing: letting my eyes readjust to the impossibly clear water and the shapes of the cryptic trout that swim beneath it. But there's also a sense of disorientation I can't quite nail down. Maybe it's a combination of disbelief that I'm actually there, such a long way physically and mentally from the home I left not a day before, coupled with the overwhelming anticipation that comes from fishing where even a typical trout is likely to be close to 2 feet long.

I came to the river's edge below a sweeping bend, where it had pushed to the edge of the floodplain and against a low bluff. On my side the bank sloped gently into gradually deepening water, while the far side carried the full force of the current almost underneath the dark green of a wall of willows. Despite the lack of sun, the reflected willows took the sheen off the surface, and with my polarised glasses to remove the remaining glare, the visibility was excellent. I took a deep breath, rechecked my knots and began to walk very slowly upstream.

At first I squinted suspiciously at every submerged branch and trout-shaped rock. I even cast to a piece of weed I had persuaded myself was moving a few inches up and down the river. In one sense you could call my slow pace and the false alarms wasted time, but in another sense I was settling in, giving my eyes time to remember what a trout looks like in a New Zealand river.

When I saw a slightly darker smudge on the bottom where a riffle spilled into a glide, I was able to confirm it was a trout because of, not in spite of, my painstaking pace: as I walked towards the shape unconvinced of its true identity, it swung about a metre to eat something, then drifted back. If I'd been striding up looking for the next hotspot, I would have missed that.

I already had a tungsten-beaded Pheasant Tail Nymph tied on beneath an indicator, so I lengthened the distance between the two to about 4 feet. The first couple of casts reminded me why it can be so important to sight these fish instead of just searching the water. Superficially, both casts were on line with the bubble trail that appeared to mirror the feeding lane the fish was occupying. But when I looked more carefully, it seemed my nymph might have been being pulled into the faster water slightly to the left of the trout. So on the third cast, I landed the fly a little to the right of the bubbles. The drift was slower, the bright green indicator went over the fish, the fish moved and I wasn't sure whether I struck because of that movement or the indicator dipping. Whichever, I was on to a brown of around 5 pounds, which immediately confirmed its size by leaping clear of the water.

It was a tremendously strong fish. That might appear to be stating the bleeding obvious, except some large New Zealand trout are manageable if you're cool-headed and patient. That wouldn't have helped with this one. It took off upstream with scary power, abruptly turned, and tore downstream. Then just as I was catching up, it bulldogged directly across the river towards a pile of willow branches on the far side. I laid my 6-weight rod on its side and bent it to the butt, trying to stop the trout burrowing into the mess. But I couldn't. I felt the first branches pluck the line like bony fingers on a guitar string, and then the trout was gone. I reeled in a broken tippet, simultaneously exhilarated and disappointed. What can you do with a fish like that?

It went on to be a magical morning, and any sting I felt from losing the first trout was soon quelled by successfully landing the next two. I caught up with Ian just as a huge fish came weaving down the river, its back and fins regularly poking from the water. We were sure it was sick or injured until we noticed it was actually feeding on duns that had abruptly started to hatch. The trout travelled 30 metres below us in the swift current, then turned and started snaking its way back upstream. Ian presented his nymph to it as it came past, but it was only interested in duns. By the time we'd both changed to dries

(Shaving Brushes) the giant trout had vanished as quickly as it had appeared.

Leaving Ian the next two bends, I headed further upstream. The burst of dun activity had motivated me to look for rising fish, and despite success to that point with the nymph, I kept the Shaving Brush on. I cut back down to the river at the tail of an idyllic dry-fly pool. It was roughly the shape of an elongated triangle, fed 100 metres upstream by a narrow and boisterous rapid, then slowly broadening toward the tail. Most of the pool looked to be 1 to 2 metres deep and the bottom was uneven due to a scattering of rocks the size of medicine balls. On the left a gravelly edge sloped in quite steeply, while on the right a vertical eroded bank, crowned with waist-high grass, plunged straight down. The main force of the current favoured the middle of the pool, but the submerged rocks caused offshoots to meander close to both banks.

The classic place for a rise was where the main bubble line slowed towards the tail of the pool. With the bumpy streambed underneath, it seemed the ideal location for a big fish to lazily chomp down the size 12 duns that were now drifting past every few seconds. I stared at the tail from a respectful distance, conscious of the fact that dun feeders can leave remarkably little disturbance — perhaps no more than a dinner-plate ring hidden among the natural swirls of current. A couple of minutes ticked by and I became more convinced that, contrary to my reasoning, no trout were feeding in the tail.

So, to sneak up which bank first? The left or the right? The current to the left of centre was somewhat gentler than the one to the right, offering any fish an easier chance at the duns. This side also featured the most defined pool 'eye' at the top — a feature beloved of New Zealand anglers as a prime lie. In favour of the right side was cover for fish, both in the form of slightly more turbulent water and the steep bank. Against it was the difficulty posed to a right-handed caster by the height of the bank plus long grass on top.

The decision was made for me when a snout the size of my hand slid briefly out of the water about halfway up the right bank. My hands began to shake and my heart sped up, yet there was a tinge of doubt. Maybe I'd only seen a tumbling piece of driftwood or the tip of a submerged rock? But a few seconds later the trout rose again, this time showing a broad back.

I waded across the thigh-deep tail to the right bank. The casting may have been easier from on top of it, but I feared my elevated profile would then alert the fish. Instead I waded against the bank, approaching to within about 10 metres of the continuing rises before the increasing depth called a halt. I'd been watching the trout the whole time, and it would rise two or three times in quick succession before vanishing for half a minute or so. It appeared that the main flow periodically pushed a fresh tongue of water (and duns) into the eddy where the trout fed. The fish rose again, snipping a little sailboard down with an audible clip. I cast quickly over my left shoulder, possibly landing the fly a few centimetres short but sure the presentation was good enough for a fish hunting the eddy for briefly stalled duns. 'Slow strike, slow strike ...' I muttered to myself as the Shaving Brush, sharply silhouetted against the steely sheen of the water, weaved through the subtle currents at the lower point of the trout's short beat. Nothing. I watched for another rise, a more precise indication of where to cast next. Then a couple of real duns twirled through the hotspot untouched and I felt the first pangs of disappointment. Had I somehow put the fish down? It wouldn't be the first time I'd spooked a New Zealand beauty notwithstanding the greatest care and caution. Some of the biggest browns seem to have an almost supernatural aptitude for sensing danger.

The seconds ticked by, but then the trout rose again. Barely had its wagging tail vanished than my fly was landing 2 metres above it — hopefully not too far up? The Shaver danced on the currents, threatening to drag. Perhaps it did, just a little, but the trout was chasing it down, jaws open as it attacked the fly from the left. Pause, lift and the fish was on.

At first the trout hung there against the bend of the rod, as if not sure whether to be annoyed or frightened. Then it pulled irresistibly upstream, taking line in short, sharp bursts. This suited me, for the trout was fighting the river as well as the rod. However, after a minute or two the fish evidently came to its senses, turned and shot downstream. I stalled the fish briefly at the pool tail, bending the butt of the rod low and sideways. Then the trout was off again, flying down the swift run below that swept to the right. Knowing I'd be better placed on the inside of the bend, I bounded back across the pool tail, rod held high. Reeling in as I moved closer to the fish, I noticed it had paused on the shallow near side of the run, facing upstream. As I approached the trout, it raced off again towards a chaotic rapid lined with flood debris. If it made the rapid and the snags, I figured my chances of landing it were slim. With little to lose, I turned the rod on its side once again and walked backwards, throwing the trout off balance for a moment. With the momentum my way, I swung the rod further back and beached the fish. Just like that.

It was the best trout I'd caught for a while, a male in superb condition, broad and deep and 8 pounds in the weigh net. It was more silver than brown, making me wonder if it had recently spent time at sea or in the estuary, which was only 50 kilometres downstream. I looked around for Ian but he was nowhere to be seen. I took a picture, then slid the fish back into the river. With hardly a beat of its tail, it drifted over the stones towards the centre of the run and vanished. I sat on a half-buried log relic from a flood long ago and took the time to look around. A few spots of rain had begun to fall lazily from the darkening sky, duns continued to drift down the bubble lines, and the tops of the cottonwoods hissed quietly in the gathering breeze. Perhaps the storm would reach us after all, but there was nowhere I'd rather have been.

SMALL STREAMS

SPRINGTIME IS SMALL stream time. They're full of water and sometimes even outsized trout that are yet to migrate down to the larger streams more in keeping with their proportions. To seal the bargain, spring flows are often higher than ideal on many of the bigger rivers, so small streams are a better bet anyway.

I might stress here that I'm talking about the really small streams, the kind that make a typical creek look like a river by comparison. You'll forgive me if I don't say exactly which ones. My mates who come with me to these little waters are always genial good company, but when we walk out after a good session, they usually say something like, 'Now you're not going to write about this creek, are you Phil?'

I should mention that these friends are more than happy to read about themselves (sometimes thinly disguised) fishing Lake Eucumbene, the Tumut or the Goulburn. But when I say they're protective of their small streams — even ones I discovered first — I mean they're protective like a mother crocodile is protective of her nest. And while I hold the view that, for many waters, it's actually a *good* thing to have lots of people trout fishing (plenty of people with a stake in fishing and habitat quality being maintained), when it comes to really little creeks, I can see my friends' point. On one tiny stream a mate and I fished recently, there was only a single decent trout in each of the few pools large enough to hold one. No more. We caught each and every one, and while each trout was also released, I doubt anyone would have found the fishing there worthwhile afterwards for a few days at least.

There's still a part of me that mistakenly thinks small streams are somehow inferior fisheries. That might be due to several childhood years when small streams were the main option — the ones I could ride a bike to or visit for a daytrip with Dad. Rivers, though, were faraway places we could only fish on long holidays. You always want what you can't have, and so in my mind bigger rivers were probably elevated further above the little waters than they deserved to be.

Some recent trips have reminded me that although some streams might be diminutive, the fishing certainly is not. For a start there's the challenge of not spooking fish when crowding bush prevents a cast from more than a rod length away. Often I find myself crawling like a wombat through tree-ferns and tea-tree to get close enough for a single bow-and-arrow cast. There are few more rewarding moments than watching your fly land where it should despite a hundred clutching plants, then having a trout take it so close you could almost touch it.

Those occasions are especially pleasing because things don't always go so well. More often, you're just about in position when you accidentally bump a stick that juts into the water or the trout somehow sees the rod tip or it simply senses something nearby is up to no good and vanishes. You're left with muddy elbows, tea-tree leaves down the back of your neck, and no fish.

Then there's the issue of landing the trout you hook. On the one hand, small stream trout are usually (though not always) comparatively small themselves. But by definition a small stream trout doesn't have to move far to find cover — often a deeply undercut bank, submerged tree roots or a pile of driftwood. A startled 1-pounder can vanish into a spaghetti of snags before you can even think 'Stop!'

Yes, although small streams can be incredibly prolific, they can also be incredibly humbling. One afternoon in north-east Tasmania recently, a friend and I must have variously lost or pricked — but mostly spooked — a hundred trout (no that's not a typo) before we actually landed one. Admittedly, the trout seemed inexplicably disinterested in feeding. Nevertheless, watching fish after fish bow-wave for cover when we were still two pools below certainly put paid to the idea of naïve little trout in pretty little streams.

Fortunately, something changed around 4 p.m. that same afternoon and the fish started feeding again. With one eye out for food, trout are never as easy to alarm and we could get close enough to present flies — which by now the fish responded to as if they were something other than a trout version of cabbage. We ended up with a respectable score before nightfall, but as we counted out a rough estimate for the diary on the muddy track back to the car, it was more with a sense of relief than victory.

Perhaps the most interesting thing about small streams is the sheer quantity of them. Few rivers simply pop up out of the ground. Instead, they begin as progressively smaller creeks unite. In wetter climates, until the absolute headwaters are reached, trout can be found. A kilometre or two below the first bogs and springs you are likely to have something large enough to hold trout. Pull out a detailed topographic map and the full extent of the small stream fishery begins to emerge. True, some will be gutters so overgrown with scrub that no amount of enthusiasm will make them fly-fishable. Then again, others will be miniature paradises so good you half wish you'd never found them in case you blurt out their location after dinner at the fly club.

My friend Malcolm and I were heading out to investigate a new stretch of small stream X recently, and we both commented on how much of it we would never see or fish, like the bits in the gorges, away from the tracks and bridges. 'The trout probably die of old age down there without ever seeing a human,' mused Malcolm as he stared off the road and into a deep valley where the mist was still burning off. 'But if we do find another good stretch, let's keep it to ourselves.'

CONFIDENCE

FEW THINGS LIFT morale on reaching a river like the sight of an early arrival already hard into a fish. As I drove along a high bank of the upper Murray River, slightly car-lagged after five solo hours on the road, brother Mark was trying to follow a large trout through knee-deep water, too busy to even notice me. By the time I'd pulled up, briefly agonised over whether to grab my gear, then run down to the water's edge without it, he was coaxing a 3-pound brown onto the shingle.

This fine display would have been a welcome sight at any time of year, but it was only October, a risky time to be visiting the upper Murray. Spring flows that are too high and too cold can really dampen the fishing this early in the season, and it was a relief to find that apparently wasn't the case this time.

Skipping formalities, as you can do with immediate family, I called out, 'What did you get him on?'

'Sink-tip line,' Mark replied distractedly, 'Peacock herl caddis grub dropper, stick caddis on the point. They're going mad for 'em.' He held the flies up briefly. From 20 metres away they were anonymous specks, but I had a fair idea what he was using. There was no need to ask the question 'How?' because Mark was already casting again. Okay — across and down, concentrating on the steps in the riffles.

Running back up the bank I grabbed my rod, rigged up about as fast as you can without risking a mistake and strode off to look for my own riffle. On the way upstream I passed our friend Jason, a relative novice, who was struggling to subdue a good trout himself. This was going to be a good session!

The next riffle seemed a facsimile of the one Mark was fishing and I approached it feeling almost guilty that it had all been worked out for me. Almost.

The first cast landed diagonally across and slightly upstream. I mended gently as the yellow floating line came past me, then a little more vigorously as it began to swing across the current below. I imagined my perfect nymphs rising slightly against the current, then feebly falling back. The strike must be imminent ... waiting, waiting. Hmmm, not that time. Let's try again.

There was no take on the second cast, nor the third. I fished the whole riffle without a touch, and somewhere in the very back of my mind a tiny voice of doubt began to whisper. But that was silly. Even the best rivers on the best days have their inexplicably quiet sections. I mentally shook myself and headed for another riffle that would surely deliver.

Just as I stepped into the edge of the river, Jason walked past. 'How're you going?' he called out.

'Oh, nothing yet but this spot looks the goods,' I replied.

'Yeah, you'll get them there. I've caught another two,' beamed Jason. 'This is the best river I've ever fished!'

I have my pride, but couldn't help myself. 'You're using that peacock herl caddis grub and stick caddis?' I asked casually.

'You bet!' he called back happily, as if it would be madness to do anything else.

Well, to cut a long and agonising story short, I fished that riffle and the next without success. I cast long and I cast short. I mended like a ribbon dancer or didn't mend at all. I swapped the order of the flies, lengthened the tippet and cut it back. Nothing helped, and at some point I began to lose faith that I would catch anything at all.

I wandered sullenly back down the river like a toddler who's missed out on the birthday cake, and found Mark. 'Well, I'm buggered if I can catch them,' I announced as if it were somehow his fault.

'Let's have a look at what you're using,' he volunteered brightly.

I showed him my flies and rig.

'Perfect!' he insisted. 'Now show me how you're fishing.'

I re-enacted the technique I'd been using for the last couple of hours.

'Yep,' said Mark, 'that's what I'm doing.'

I wasn't sure if this was what I wanted to hear or not, but I'd suddenly had enough of wet-fly fishing. 'Think I'll head back to the car and wait until they start rising,' I announced with a trace of petulance.

'Okay,' said Mark evenly, 'but why don't you have one more go up at the big bend opposite the poplars. That has to be the nicest run on the river at this height.'

'All right,' I sighed, 'I'll give it a try.'

The 15-minute walk up to the bend gave me time to reflect, not least on the fact that I'm always telling others to persevere so perhaps I should take some of my own advice. I drew a deep breath and strode over the river rocks to the top of the poplar run. I don't know if it was the way the riffly bend gently curved around me, or a change in attitude, but the water had a different feel to it. As I cast across the current and mended the line, I experienced a renewed belief that something might actually eat my flies.

The invisible nymphs cruised past me and I felt the slightest tick through the line as one or other briefly tapped the bottom. Then just as the line was about to swing in the current, it stopped. I lifted the rod with that mixture of hope and caution a few fishless hours can create, and a 4-pound brown took off downstream.

I won't pretend to recall the blur of what happened next, but eventually I beached the magnificent fish on a sandbar way down river. Once satisfied the trout was safely landed, I looked up to see if anyone had witnessed my breakthrough, but Mark and Jason were nowhere to be seen. I walked back up to the top of the poplar bend and started again. This time it took two casts before I hooked up and the downstream chase recommenced.

Over the next hour I caught more large Australian river trout in a session than ever before or since. I won't talk exact sizes and numbers because a few years on I scarcely believe the figures myself so I can hardly expect you to! But I do recall the almost mystical faith I soon developed that the riffle was stacked with trout like sleepers on a railway, and with every cast another strike was imminent. The amazing thing was that I never saw a single fish until it was on my line. It was almost as if by power of imagination they were there and I would catch them.

Now, if only I could re-create that feeling every time I'm on the water ...

SPONTANEITY

THE PHONE RANG at 7.30 on a sunny October morning. Calls that early usually mean either bad news, or an overseas friend or relative with their time zone confused. Fortunately, it was neither of these. Instead, it was Muz Wilson with a fishing report so urgent it couldn't wait for a more civilised hour.

Phone calls from Muz had become more frequent as winter had moved into spring, and the fishing in both his local lakes — Bullen Merri and Purrumbete — had picked up. But then there had been a subtle shift from the mere reporting of some good fishing. As time went on and I'd continually failed to front for the splendid sport Muz was constantly describing, he must have come to the understandable conclusion that I was a little thick. He began to add things to his reports like 'This won't last forever', and 'It would be a shame to miss it.'

Not surprisingly, with this most recent call, Muz spelled out what he had been leading up to for some months. As if patiently explaining an important mathematical fact to a distracted child, Muz told me how, just the previous day, he had polaroided at least 50 trout at Purrumbete. This day was shaping up to be even better, he said, with a cloudless sky and light wind. Therefore, he was taking the boat out on the lake again and he strongly suggested I join him. After all, Muz continued, I was only a 90-minute drive away. He finished by pointedly noting that blue-sky days weren't exactly abundant during the Western District spring.

These days, my spur-of-the-moment fishing trips are rarer events than they used to be. I fish as often as ever, and I manage to duck out for a couple of unplanned hours with pleasing frequency. But trips of significance are normally written on the calendar at least a few days — and often a few months — in advance. And that's after a bit of date-juggling between me and whoever I'm going away with. My immediate thought as I listened to Muz was that there must inevitably be something to stop me going fishing for a whole day at such short notice.

But as I scanned the calendar and gestured questions to my partner Jane, I began to realise that there was no reason I couldn't go to Purrumbete as soon as I finished breakfast. Or at least there wasn't a reason that couldn't be dealt with via a couple of phone calls and some hard work later in the week.

An hour later, I was heading south-west across the Western District plains, flushed green with spring growth. The Camperdown area vies even with Ballarat for lack of sunshine and I hoped Muz's weather report would hold. It did, and as the crater-lake landmark of Mount Leura appeared in the distance, the clouds remained as scarce as Red Tags in an end-of-season fly box. I called Muz to tell him I was nearly there. 'Good,' he replied, and I heard some rustling sounds as he no doubt attempted to readjust the phone on his shoulder while stripping in a fly. 'Got a nice brownie a few minutes ago,' he continued, and managed not to add 'already'.

Soon after, I was climbing aboard Muz's new boat. As we headed across the sparkling ripple to the north-west shore, I had a few minutes to reflect on how my day had changed from two hours earlier. But not for long. In no time, Muz had started the electric motor and we were gliding silently along, a decent cast out from shore. The steep bank in the background pasted a generous glare-free strip on the water, and at any point we could see into at least half an acre of lake. Yet besides a single shape darting beneath the boat, we saw nothing for the first 100 metres — just long enough to cast the tiniest doubt that something wasn't right.

And then suddenly, there were the trout. Often, not merely *a* trout, but four or five, all visible at once. Most were 3-pounders, with a sprinkling of fish twice that size adding to the shaky-knees factor. As always in such clear water so brightly lit, the fish were difficult. The inshore cruisers were easiest to see but hardest to fool. They were nervous and flighty, and sometimes leading the fish by 10 metres was still too close. Muz came nearest to success. A perfect ambush in the shade of a willow had one fat brownie literally chewing on his inert damsel nymph, but Muz lost sight of the fish in a patch of glare at the crucial moment, and I was too slow to call the strike.

The trout working the holes and channels in the milfoil weed further offshore were a little harder to see but more obliging. I half-heartedly covered one 3-pounder with the Scintilla Stick Caddis as it appeared to flee the boat. But then the fish turned on the plip just as a wind gust brought the boat racing towards it. The trout nearly crashed into the hull as it engulfed the fly.

And so it went with one of the most thrilling days I've enjoyed for ages. Too soon, we were forced to reluctantly accept that the sun was too low to see the fish in time. It seemed that the hours had evaporated in mere minutes. The only clue to the real length of time we had spent on the water was a back-count of the number of fish sighted. Muz and I agreed that we must have polaroided at least 60 *different* trout — so that's not counting fish we think we saw more than once.

I was tired from an intense day, which was added to by a long, solo drive home. But when I walked in the door that night, I made a special point of pulling out the fishing diary and writing the trip up. If I'd waited a few days, I might have struggled to recall the exact date — it wasn't written anywhere on the calendar.

LOSING FISH

WHILE I CAN recall a fair bit about most of the large fish I've successfully landed, nothing quite burns into the memory like a big fish lost. My big fish tragedies are not confined to seasons; in fact, I wouldn't have any difficulty coming up with several for each month of the year, so I initially struggled with where to place this chapter. But bear with me while we temporarily leave spring for an autumn from years gone by.

I calculate that it was about 30 years ago when I was fishing up from the Glen Valley Bridge on the upper Mitta Mitta River. It was a late May morning and in my enthusiasm I had headed off from camp way too early. Thick frost carpeted the grass and glazed the trees in glitter. Puddles by the roadside were frozen solid.

The river itself steamed, and even as a teenager I had already learned that this was not a good sign. Sure enough, for the first hour or so the sharply clear water seemed devoid of all life. Then as I neared local farmer Jack Batty's open paddocks, the sun finally crept over the shoulder of Mount Wills and brought a tinge of warmth to the wintry landscape. Encouragingly, a few midges now lazily buzzed above the water though there was still no sign of a trout.

I fished on for another hour, casting a large brown nymph into all the likely places, but nothing. The air was now sufficiently warm that the ice was melting from the overhanging trees and dripping into the river like light rain. After working an appealing pool for no result, I moved on to the run above. A large, bleached tree trunk lay in the middle and parallel to the current. It was a likely spot, but with so many fine lies explored without result, I had lost that crucial belief that a trout would eat my fly. So I was fishing robotically beside the old log when the line went tight. For a moment, I assumed the nymph was snagged, but then came that unmistakable throb of a living thing.

There are some very good trout in the upper Mitta of today, and that was certainly the case in the 1970s. I knew by the weight through the rod that I had hooked one of these. Inevitably, the unseen trout pulled for the sanctuary of the log, but somehow I managed to turn it. The trout then raced downstream, so I followed it into the quieter pool below. At that point, things were looking promising. While the big brown circled, I was already plotting my return to camp, walking down the gravel road to the tents with my prize — 4 pounds at least — proudly borne on a strong stick.

As luck would have it, a cheap short-handled aluminum net, brand new, dangled from an elastic strap around my shoulder. This was the first time I had ever carried a net, and I blessed my good sense. The moment the trout passed within reach, I swiped. There was a lot of splashing, followed by heavy weight through the handle, and I lifted. But then the instant of glory was replaced by a long second of horror. The trout was not safely in the net; it was dangling on the outside. The exposed point of the nymph hook had snagged the mesh. I gaped helplessly at the biggest trout I'd ever caught, before summoning enough sense to desperately flip the net under it. Alas, as I began to act, the trout gave a mighty heave and back into the river it fell. I remember the futile dive after it with the net, the faint hope as I felt something catch on the rim, and then the ultimate desolation as I realised it was only a branch. My arms were soaked in freezing water up to the elbows. Sitting here now, decades later, I can vividly recall the faintly mossy smell of the river silt as I wrung out my sleeves.

If there's one thing worse than losing your own fish, it's quite possibly losing someone else's. Here I must delve even further into my past, to when I was the impressionable age of twelve. I was surf fishing a wild beach near Peterborough on Victoria's west coast with Dad and our regular fishing companions, the Julian family. After a quiet morning, the patriarch of the Julian clan, John, hooked a ripper. Slowly and skilfully he fought a salmon of at least 6 pounds into the wash, at which point I suddenly and without invitation decided to render assistance. I ran down the steep beach and grabbed at the flapping fish, which promptly found the strength for one more mighty heave, then disappeared out of my arms and into the froth. I attended John's 80th birthday recently and although he outwardly chuckled upon recalling this incident (I had the feeling he didn't have to dig very deep in the memory bank) his laugh had a hollow ring to it.

Sufficiently chastened by the Peterborough episode, I've managed to avoid losing other people's big fish ever since, although guiding has forced some close calls. In case I needed any extra motivation to stay away, where possible, from the trophies of others, a friend recently failed to fit another friend's trout of a lifetime into his way-too-small net. These two don't agree about much anymore, but they do agree that the trout in question was around 12 pounds.

When it comes to losing my own trout without any help, there are two distinct categories of loss, and there's a certain morbid fascination in trying to decide which is worse. The first category is the plain old stuff-up. These range from small mistakes, like failing to remove a wind-knot in the tippet, through to the more grandiose such as falling over mid-fight, or that showstopper, the panicked net swipe — as per the Mitta incident recently described. The net swipe can either cut through the tippet or briefly and tantalisingly leave the trout teetering on the wrong side of the net frame. If your pride isn't dented enough already, you can then chase after the escaped fish, flailing at the water like a deranged butterfly collector. I don't know of anyone who has ever recaptured a fleeing fish this way but you could always be the first.

The second category of fish loss concerns the big one that gets away for no good reason. In contrast to the stuff-up, your knots are good and you play the trout as coolly as you can when you're attached to the sort of fish you might never have a chance at again. Everything's going well. The runs are becoming shorter; the fish is showing on the surface more often. You're probably beginning to back up towards the bank, maybe even thinking about getting a photo. There won't be any mistakes with the net. And then the line is suddenly slack.

My first thought at this moment is always 'That can't be right.' Even when all the evidence is to the contrary, for a second or two I assume the line has somehow slipped through my fingers or off the reel and I didn't notice, or the fish is swimming towards me. There follows some frantic stripping to gather the slack, but the crushing reality soon sinks in. The fish has gone.

So which is worse? Losing a special fish that a post-mortem reveals you could have landed if you'd done things differently, or losing one which, in all modesty, you deserved to catch? I still haven't quite worked that one out, but meanwhile, there's another issue to consider, and that's the appropriate response.

The finer traditions of flyfishing would have the angler taking the loss of a big'un on the chin, so to speak. The only sign of disappointment might be a slight shake of the head, but this would be quickly followed by a wry grin and perhaps a philosophical pronouncement like 'That's why we call it fishing, not catching.'

Well, call me petulant, but about the only time I can salute the one that got away is when I've safely landed a beauty or two beforehand. A couple of Octobers ago I lost what was probably the largest river trout I've ever had on my line. It was a category two loss: when I replayed the fight in my mind (and, believe me, I did this a lot) I couldn't think of anything I might have done differently. There were a few occasions when the huge brown must have come close to breaking the line on rocks and logs. I could have coped with that, because there simply wouldn't have been any way to prevent it. But in the event, it was when the worst was over and I finally had the fish on the surface that the nymph popped out of its mouth. There was actually a fleeting moment when the trout just lay there, unaware it was free. If the water between us hadn't been 10 feet deep I would have definitely attempted a net swipe. "#@%$!" I yelled, in a way that had more in common (I assume) with John McEnroe than David Scholes. I managed to restrain myself from hurling the rod onto the rocks. However, I did sit down and sulk in a way that would have done the players in the *Brat Camp* television series proud.

A couple of years on, I'm beginning to get over it. The thing I'm still trying to understand though is why it bothers me so much when an exceptional fish gets away. Of course I like catching a big one, but I'm not a trophy hunter. Often when choosing destinations, I'll happily trade a shot at a monster for other things, like lots of action, or scenery, or the company of the right people. But perhaps it simply comes down to this: if landing a big fish is a thrill, then losing one has to be a disappointment.

SUMMER

MITTA MOMENTS

THE HUME FREEWAY has two redeeming features: it takes southern Victorians like me part of the way towards the mountain streams of the north-east, and it takes us there fairly quickly. The Hume's original surveyors knew what they were doing sacrificing scenery for speed. In staying away from the foothills wherever possible and sticking resolutely to the dreary plains below, the Hume is undeniably efficient, heading north without a single low-speed bend or truck-congested climb.

Efficient maybe, but it's a boring drive on your own. By the time I reached the halfway township of Euroa to rendezvous with fellow anglers Max and Eddie and travel on to the Mitta Mitta River, the summer holiday radio options were wearing thin.

Euroa is a pretty town, just close enough to the granite hills of the Strathbogie Ranges to capture some of their charm. There are also red gums, a large creek and, most significantly for me, a friend Robyn's garage where I can leave my car (or mates can leave theirs) when we meet up to share the remaining few hours' drive to the mountains.

Today Euroa was lethargic under a relentless January sun, blinds drawn and side streets deserted. It felt vaguely incongruous to unload rods and fishing gear for cold-water trout onto Robyn's baking lawn.

There was barely time to check I hadn't left something important behind when Max and Eddie pulled up. We had departed from points 100 kilometres apart to converge within minutes. This is the sort of punctuality I appreciate on a fishing trip. While time cheerfully dissolves into the abstract when you're thigh deep in a summer river, it moves slowly when you're sitting on dying grass in 40°C heat.

The journey had scarcely missed a beat and we were back on the Hume again. The arrow-straight bitumen became a mere backdrop as talk quickly turned to the days ahead. Max and I had both received a vague SMS from Al and Dale, who had already been fishing the mountain streams for two days. The message simply showed a picture of Dale holding a brown trout that looked about 4 pounds, with a glimpse of clear, rocky water in the background. No details, no place names.

Past Glenrowan, we turned east off the Hume. It is here you first see the real mountains, those over 1500 metres, snow-capped in winter. But they're vague and distant, with perspective reducing the tallest peaks as they struggle to peer from behind lesser ones. Almost as soon as you leave the freeway you're technically in the valley of the Ovens, a river that becomes a trout stream further up, although here it winds its silty way across a flat, straw-coloured plain.

Only as you continue to progress east do humble hills begin to define the valley's edges. Gradually, these grow taller and come closer, until soon after passing through the town of Myrtleford, you are in very different country to that left on the Hume a mere 40 minutes earlier. To reinforce the point, Myrtleford roughly marks the beginning of trout water — beyond here, trout can be caught in the Ovens River and its tributaries more often than not.

You only have to drive a little further before the mountains occupy so much of the landscape that roads can only travel so far in any direction before they must climb up and over. Faced with the direct but tortuous climb over Tawonga Gap or the slight detour through the less demanding Happy Valley (yes, it's really called that), Max opted for the latter. This route brought us alongside the Kiewa River as night was falling. We contemplated pulling over at one of the bridges to try the last of the evening rise, but then recalled how chaotic and usually futile it is to set up to fish with only minutes of usable light. We decided to push on.

Soon after, we left the last of the Kiewa flats at Mount Beauty and began the long twisting climb up to Falls Creek Village and the Bogong High Plains. Towering alpine ash forest closed in, and our visible world constricted to the beam of the headlights as they swung from one tree-fern-studded embankment to the next. A sambar deer doe and fawn nonchalantly crossed the road just ahead. A few more bends and we could glimpse Falls Creek up above, its twinkling lights mingling with the stars.

Beyond Falls Creek we reached the top of the Bogong High Plains and the gradient flattened out. Night and altitude, approaching 1700 metres, had banished the heat. Off to our right, Rocky Valley Reservoir was a dark mass on a black night. Rocky Valley teems with trout and there would be fish rising by the hundred on a night like this. Yes, there's a lot of good water to drive past on trips to the upper Mitta, which is why many flyfishers never quite get there.

At least it was a clear night crossing the high plains. Pea-soup fog on these treeless moors is common after dark, an unwelcome obstacle following many hours' driving. I recalled one night so foggy I was forced to walk ahead of the car to look for cattle asleep on the warm road while my companion drove.

We began the descent into the Mitta Mitta Valley. Once more the road became a slot through thick forest. Wombats ambled along the verge; possums scurried up bark that glowed white in the headlights. There was a glimpse of a larger animal ahead, perhaps another deer?

Active wildlife after dark often follows a good evening's fishing, and as we drove the final kilometres to the huts that would be our home for the next few days, we speculated on what stories Al and Dale would have for us about the fishing we'd missed. Before long the smell of grass and horses carried on the night air outside, the soft glow of gas lamps appeared ahead, and we were there.

Including Anthony (who'd arrived independently that afternoon) there were six of us for coffee in the hut that evening. Six anglers can be four too many on a flyfishing trip, but find the right location and, most importantly, the right people and it can work. On the first count, the upper Mitta system has so much water that there are still bits of the main river I haven't got around to yet despite 30 years of trips, not to mention parts of the tributaries like the Cobungra, Bundara, Livingstone and Victoria.

As for the company, I'd fished with all the party before except Anthony and knew I would happily fish with any of them again. It didn't take long to work out that Anthony would be easy to share a stream with too.

Assessing what makes people fun to go away with is to risk dancing on the edge of conceit — you need only consider that they're making their own decisions about *you* to appreciate that. Still, I will say that I liked how everyone was there primarily to fish, rather than, say, sleep or drink beer. At the same time, catching fish wasn't life and death. Nobody seemed to mind whom they fished with or which stretch of water they ended up on. I would have been surprised if any most-fish/biggest-fish braggers had been invited, and none was. On the domestic front, things seemed to get done around camp with a minimum of fuss. No one appeared to have forgotten that their mother wasn't along to look after them. Dale and Max did more than their fair share of the cooking, but they were very good at it and seemed to enjoy it. The rest of us responded by quietly attempting to keep the dishes and table in some sort of order.

The fishing turned out to be very good. The valleys were green, and signs of the 2003 wildfire that incinerated the whole area were hard to find. I remembered the deathly silent landscape of white ash and charcoaled trees that had stretched to the horizon only five short years earlier, and marvelled at the recovery.

The streams were flowing at ideal height for summer, just licking at the swordgrass fronds that draped the edges. The summer heat was tempered by thunderstorms that swelled like rolls in an oven every afternoon. Thunderstorms can make or ruin summer fishing in the mountains and we tracked their progress with a mixture of anxiety and excitement.

The first morning I teamed with Max to fish a remote section of the river and we enjoyed modest success. Then, as the clouds began to build, and the still air vibrated with distant thunder, we rendezvoused with Dale and Eddie, and headed for a stretch of water where the road and the car would be close by if the storm forced a retreat. This time, Dale and I fished together, by which I mean we leapfrogged up the same stretch and occasionally cast side-by-side where the river was wide enough.

The narrow sky grew darker and the thunder nearer. In these deep, forested valleys, it is difficult to pick the direction and size of approaching thunderheads, so we fished on and hoped. As expected, the trout seemed to be invigorated by the dynamic conditions. Rises began to appear more frequently and even blind casts to likely riffles and pockets drew a share of takes. By now I was fishing with a Wee Creek Hopper, partly because of the numerous grasshoppers bouncing in the riverside grass, but mostly because Max had radioed he'd caught a brace of 2-pounders on the same fly an hour earlier.

I'd soon landed some nice browns between a pound and two, and judging by Dale's egret-like stance a few hundred metres upstream, he was also having action. Still the thunder rumbled and solitary drops of rain the size of pebbles occasionally splatted beside me from the swirling sky. I couldn't tell whether the storm was yet to hit us or passing by.

I arrived at the tail of a pool broad enough and deep enough to absorb the Mitta's considerable flow, so the surface was flat and barely moving. Normally I skip these stretches. The feeding lanes are ill-defined or non-existent, and on this afternoon there was no hope of sighting a cruising fish in the poor light. Then in the deep water on the far bank, beneath a crumbling slope of scree and loose tussocks, a trout rose. The rise was at once interesting and meaningless — too far away to cover quickly, and removed from any bubble lines or current seams that could give some predictability to the trout's position. Then it rose again, about 3 metres upstream, and suddenly there was hope.

Two rises in a giant, near flow-less pool might prove to be a mere flash in the pan, the trout then vanishing for the rest of the day. But there was a chance the fish was being more deliberate, working a beat at the base of the steep slope for hoppers or other terrestrials tumbling in. So I waded as far towards the rises as I could (about a third of the way across) and delivered a 20-metre cast. The Wee Creek landed with a gentle plop about two rod lengths upstream of the last rise, and began an almost imperceptible drift along the bank. For a few seconds I was poised to strike, but as the fly dawdled a metre, then two with no sign of the fish, I quickly lost confidence. I was actually looking upriver and planning the next move, my peripheral vision barely tracking the little fawn dot of the Wee Creek, when it disappeared in a loud rise. I lifted the rod instantly, knowing there would be a delay in hitting the fish because of the distance between us. The strike came up tight, and a decent brown shot from the water beside the scree bank.

I couldn't believe my luck, but there would be time to contemplate that later; meanwhile a very strong fish was pulling determinedly for some logs I hadn't noticed before. With the last few coils of fly line revealing the yellow backing beneath, my control over the trout felt uncomfortably delayed and vague, as if an action on my part took seconds to actually transmit to the fish. Nevertheless, I must have turned it before the logs, because next thing the trout was heading down towards the tail of the pool. This was a positive as the shallower water was visibly clear of line-snagging sticks. However, the trout soon sensed the quickening current and used it to make a rush for the pool tail and the rapids below. Laying the rod sideways and bending it against the fish, I managed to swivel it in an arc that transcribed a dangerous pass across the lip of the tail, then into the quieter water on my side.

Finally the trout seemed under control. It tried a couple of crocodile rolls as big trout often do, but it was close to me now and I could apply just the right amount of pressure to avoid any nasty outcomes. Next thing I knew, the trout was in the net — a female brown over 3 pounds, dotted with big black spots like a leopard. I could see Dale fishing the run below, about 100 metres downstream. I lifted the fish in the net and waved, but Dale was still egret-like, focused only on the stretch of water in front of him. (I learned later that he'd caught three fish from it.) 'Hey Dale,' I yelled above the rapids, 'Got a nice one!'

He looked up and I lifted the fish in my hands before releasing it. Dale generously gave a thumbs-up, although at that range I could have been holding up a piece of wood and he wouldn't have known the difference. The drops of rain were falling more densely, and I noticed I was starting to get wet. I sought shelter beneath a thick tree leaning out from the bank and listened to the plop of the raindrops turn into a loud hiss. Dale kept casting.

The good fishing continued, although just a few kilometres upriver Max barely made it back to the car before it was pounded by marble-sized hailstones. Somewhere up in the mountains, a true deluge sent a flush of dirty water down the river, discolouring the pools as we watched. However, it must have been extremely localised, as the river began to clear within the hour and the fishing never really missed a beat.

As happens on great fishing trips (or maybe any fishing trip) the next couple of days passed too quickly. On the last evening as Max and Dale conjured up a seafood pasta feast by headlamp and portable stove, the discussion turned to the next day. As the farm horses chewed softly in the dark outside the door, we considered our options. Stay and fish the Mitta 'til the last moment or break the trip home with some time on the Kiewa? Al had left already and Anthony had packed away his rod for a dawn departure and long solo drive home. The remaining four of us couldn't decide, and so we chose to fish the Mitta the next morning; we'd pull out for the Kiewa if it were quiet.

Of course that was never likely to happen. The morning did begin unspectacularly, but we were fishing a river that had produced consistently for two days and I found myself aimlessly pondering just how bad the fishing would have to be before we'd give it up.

If the chances of a Kiewa visit were slim to begin with, they were gone by mid morning. By then a warm sun had the hoppers hopping and the cicadas chirping so loudly you couldn't hear the rises properly. The fishing got better and better, or at least the catching did — the sport was marred a little by the fact that Dale and I had misjudged our beat, so we were literally jogging from pool to pool, trying not to miss the best spots before the clock ran out. I know, we could have worked on Max and Eddie staying out longer than the agreed meeting time of 2 p.m., but the truth was they were more likely to honour our agreement and forego good fishing by waiting for us on the roadside.

Dale broke off a trout in the final run (couldn't tell if it was a tippet weakness or an outsized fish), and shouted he just had to have a few more casts to redeem the situation. I caught a sighted $1\frac{1}{2}$-pounder in the anabranch opposite, released it, and strode through the scrub to the road. Sure enough, Max and Eddie drove up just as I stepped onto the gravel.

'Hard to leave, eh?' said Max shaking his head sympathetically.

'Yeah, and I think we might have to wrestle Dale back to the car,' I added, but just then he burst out of the forest, sweating and slightly scratched.

The morning was, of course, over too soon. Yet already, as the car wound along the road above the river and towards our distant homes, the talk was turning to a return visit in a couple of months, and the vague feeling of something lost forever began to fade.

MEAL TIME

A TRIP LIKE the Mitta one just described reinforces the somewhat confused relationship I have with food when fishing. Under the direction of Max and Dale, the Mitta catering was taken pretty seriously, with the party as a whole regarding the meals as more than just something to keep you alive between casts. The mornings began with the aroma of freshly brewed coffee mingling with the river-flat mist (instant coffee was banned). Breakfast was lashings of bacon and poached eggs, the latter being a personal favourite which I always muck up on my own.

Lunches were foccacias or pita breads, individually wrapped and crammed with a bewildering but delicious range of fillings. They were so good that on at least one occasion I remained seated on a river rock finishing mine while a decent trout rose 5 metres away. As for the evening meals, these hit new heights for camp food, especially given the difficult conditions under which they were prepared. Max and Dale's team effort of T-bones with field mushrooms and pan-fried chips, prepared on a hotchpotch of tiny camp stoves by inadequate light, was close to miraculous.

There have been other trips that I can effortlessly recall for the food, notwithstanding competition from outstanding fishing. I don't think I've ever enjoyed a succession of meals as much as I did at Cape York aboard Carpentaria Seafaris' *Tropic Paradise*. I adore seafood, and of course much of what we ate on board was not only unquestionably fresh but exotic too. I mentioned the longtail tuna sashimi in an earlier chapter, but the Spanish mackerel fish and chips and chilli mud crab were equally unforgettable. At my friend Felix's Owen River Lodge in New Zealand, I've managed to blend in with the paying guests and enjoy Jude's seafood bouillabaisse, not to mention her braised venison and other local treats. Sometimes though, it is the simplest fare that brings the most wistful post-trip smile, like Ross's smoked trout, eaten on crackers after a blissful day on Arthurs Lake, Tasmania.

Yes, there's no denying how much I enjoy good food and I can't go long without sustenance of some description. However, in some sort of cosmic mistake, I'm not much of a meal planner or cook. Both failings are highlighted over the summer months, when the long days can cause nine or ten hours to pass between lunch and an after-dark dinner. Part of the problem is my goldfish-like memory when it comes to hunger. When I'm foodless and half-starving in the summer twilight, I vow and declare I will never put myself in the same predicament again. I silently promise I'll load my vest with goodies and the esky with the finest foods as soon as I get back to base. But no sooner have I eaten than my brush with starvation fades to a half-forgotten discomfort ... until the next time.

To compound this predicament, I've somehow managed to choose several fishing companions who can skip lunch without a second thought. When they finally get around to cooking, mates like Lindsay, Peter and Mick can prepare superb meals. But most of the time they regard eating as an afterthought, something they do occasionally because they're dimly aware that if they didn't they would eventually die.

Lunch-less and giddy with hunger at about 3 p.m. one afternoon on St Clair Lagoon in Tasmania, I suggested to Lindsay that, having not eaten since our dawn patrol breakfast, we might like to pop back to the cabin for a feed. The huge rise to black spinners, I added, would probably still be going when we got back. Lindsay looked at me as if I'd suggested he break his rod over his knee. What happened after that is a blur, but I think I survived by eating handfuls of emerging nymphs and a raw trout.

When it comes to shopping (assuming I remember to) and preparing good food on a fishing trip, I'll confess my efforts can sometimes favour the pragmatic over the stylish. On a recent outing, one of my friends suggested that my simple but hearty provisions — ham and cheese sandwiches — weren't exactly what he'd had in mind for the evening meal. He was similarly underwhelmed the next night on finding tinned sausage and vegetables on the menu, even after I pointed out that this was not only a nutritious meal, but one that had the advantage of being heated and served within minutes of our late return from the evening rise.

But lest I be judged too harshly around the camp kitchen, I must tell a story from my student days about a meal I prepared of which I'm still proud. Money was always tight on those early fishing trips, so imagine my delight when visiting the butcher's shop in Wangaratta en route to the Kiewa River grasshopper feeders, to find that not only was lamb's fry on special, but also that universal favourite, brains. Poker-faced, I concealed this win from my three angling mates, hinting only that I'd be cooking a special camp meal the next evening.

Sure enough, the following day I dragged myself away from the Kiewa before the evening rise to begin preparing dinner. Using only a poorly lit camp stove, I cooked the lamb's fry and brains, then in a stroke of culinary genius, added a can of tomatoes. I left this masterpiece to simmer while my mates returned one by one from the river.

I couldn't read the expressions of my friends properly by lamplight, but they seemed pleasantly surprised, even astonished, as they tucked in.

'What do you call this then?' asked Luke.

'Liver Surprise,' I announced with a slight flourish.

'What's the surprise?' enquired Tom in his usual deadpan voice.

'The brains,' I answered proudly. '*And* they were on special.'

Everyone looked up from their bowls with a stare I took to be admiration, then Tom suddenly got up and disappeared into the dark, probably to find a suitable bottle of red — although he was gone a while. Anyway, my efforts were so appreciated that the boys insisted they do the cooking for the rest of the trip. In fact, they still insist all these years later, despite my feeble protests. To be honest though, I'm secretly glad — I doubt I could ever better my Liver Surprise.

THE FOOD CHAIN

MICK AND I have swapped trout flies for something a little bigger and brighter, and decided to try for mid-summer salmon off Queenscliff, on the central Victorian coast. We're in the company of Steve Stojanovski, co-owner of Firstcast Fishing Adventures. Steve is a mate of Mick's, and Mick has persuaded me to join them. Persuaded, as in 'Steve's clients have been catching stacks of good salmon on the fly. Would you like to come along Monday afternoon?'

Mercifully, Monday afternoon is blank on the calendar and the three of us are soon boarding Steve's boat at the Swan Bay ramp. Despite my limited knowledge of things nautical, I note with appreciation that the craft is much bigger than his four-wheel drive, and apparently weighs more than 2 tonnes. I have a newfound fondness for large, sturdy boats, having recently spent a couple of precarious hours squid fishing in what was more or less a motorised bathtub.

We cruise quietly alongside the moored boats in the channel leading out of Swan Bay, and then abruptly enter the vastness of Port

Phillip. After a bushfire scorcher 48 hours earlier, it's a beautiful clear day, cooled by a modest southerly. The bay is deep blue as ocean water arrives through The Rip, a narrow entrance only a few kilometres south. There's a mixture of swell and chop, but the incoming tide is in harmony with the wind, and the bow cuts comfortably through the waves.

Steve expertly steers the boat, but his actions on the controls are almost automatic as he sweeps hundreds of hectares of water for telltale signs of salmon. Here and there, gannets fall like javelins, but the activity is patchy and short lived. Eventually, Steve races the boat towards a small, agitated cluster of birds. They're gone within moments of our arrival, but Steve gets us to cast to one side of where the birds were. The first presentation with a chartreuse Clouser is in vain. But halfway back on the second cast, a faster strip is rewarded with a hard bump. Moments later, there's weight on the end — an instant of firm resistance —and then a fish screams away. It leaps twice, and sure enough it's a salmon. The fish is a little under 2 pounds, but it bends the rod as hard as most species twice that size.

Soon Mick is into a similar fish, and then we lose the school. But it's nice to be 'on the board', and there's a distinct lift in confidence. Steve finds a couple more patches of salmon over the next hour, and the tally slowly climbs. This is good fishing, no doubt about it, and Mick and I are already laughing at the slightest excuse and giving each other a hard time about casting slip-ups, 'trout strikes', and fish lost at the boat — the sort of banter absent on tough days. Steve is happy enough, but you can tell he's not satisfied. Those shaded eyes keep sweeping the water far away, even as we're landing fish in close.

And suddenly, his expression changes. 'Jeez, look over there!' he cries, pointing towards a distant cliff. At first I see nothing, but then I realise that the dots of confetti highlighted against the shaded cliff are seabirds.

'Wind in and sit down,' urges Steve, and guns the motor. The big boat cuts through the chop, and in minutes we're just two long casts from the cliff. I've never seen anything like it. Hundreds of birds are squawking, diving and snatching.

'See the krill?' shouts Steve above the noise. A dark-maroon stain colours the water for about 100 metres by 50, the inner edge almost touching the shore. Somewhere beneath it, the whitebait are feasting. And here and there, the surface boils like a rapid in flood as the salmon attack the whitebait. It's a primal scene — something I'd expect to see in a remote Cape York bay, not a long throw from million-dollar bayside homes.

Steve expertly manoeuvres the boat to hover within a comfortable cast of the outer edge of the chaos. I'm frantic to throw in a fly, though it soon becomes obvious this session is going to last. Earlier, retrieve and fly depth had to be pretty right. Now it seems the salmon, worked to frenzy, will attack anything. My first few careful presentations are hit so recklessly that I soon catch some nice fish, and I begin to experiment. In less than 2 metres of water I can actually watch the salmon respond to the fly. On one cast, I don't even move the Clouser after it lands, yet it barely has time to sink a few inches when a huge salmon rockets up from the bottom to annihilate it. Unfortunately, an even more desperate fish, slightly smaller, zooms across the surface and beats it. As I wrestle it, I shake my head at the absurdity of thinking 'Oh no!' as a 4-pound salmon eats my fly.

Mick realises sooner than I that the clock is on our side this time. He can afford to take a few moments to change from sinking line to floater and attach a surface popper. The results are instantly spectacular. As Mick jerks the bright green fly across the water, salmon after salmon gets half airborne fighting for the right to eat it. Eventually one wins about a metre from the boat and Mick's distinctive laugh competes with the cries of the gulls and terns.

The popper looks like fun, but I can't bring myself to change fly line and fly. Just a couple more casts with the Clouser ... However, if I can't actually bear to stop fishing long enough to change rigs, I can now take the time to fully appreciate where I am and what's going on. The live, giant food chain is no longer the background — it becomes as much my focus as the fishing. The gannets are the most spectacular predator above the surface. I read once that they sometimes hit the water at 100 kilometres per hour and only survive the impact because they have a reinforced skull. The salmon seem more unruly, darting here and there in an apparently disorganised way. But every one we catch has a distended stomach, and often 4-inch whitebait spewing from their mouths. Unruly or not, the salmon are proving ruthlessly effective at catching the baitfish.

It's simultaneously a brutal and beautiful scene, carnage and life, and although I release most of my catch, in a way I'm part of it. For a moment I think of people who don't fish, and feel sorry for them.

BLOWING IN THE WIND

THE PROPERTY WHERE I live is known as Windy Hill. It seems that's
what it has always been called, despite the best efforts of the local real
estate agent to conceal the fact when we first visited the property. 'It's
not windy *really*,' the agent said through a fixed grin when I playfully
enquired about the name. 'More a regular, refreshing breeze.'

Looking back, I wonder if buying a property called Windy Hill was
an act of subconscious bravado for a flyfisher. There's also the
possibility that, on some level, I imagined living on a hilltop beset by
gales might acclimatise me to wind to the point where I became
benignly indifferent to it.

Well, Windy Hill has lived up to its name. I doubt even our agent
friend from all those years ago would be able to call the mini-typhoon
that rocks the house as I type 'refreshing' — not without looking at his
feet anyway! But, a touch disappointingly, it turns out that a decade
of exposure to fierce gales has done little to affect my uneasy
relationship with wind when fishing.

A trip to Tasmania during late summer reinforced this love–hate relationship. The first day, a near hurricane drove Neil, Lindsay and me from the highlands. However the tempest up top proved a perfect grasshopper wind on the lowland streams. The gusts were strong enough to deposit dozens of hapless hoppers on the water, but not sufficiently powerful or constant to compromise our casting.

A plague of hoppers and a decent breeze produced the kind of textbook fishing we spend most of summer dreaming about but actually encounter less often. This day, hoppers weren't just a part of the trout's diet or even an important part of the trout's diet: they were *the* diet. Trout chose feeding lies dictated foremost by hopper supply and responded to presentations primarily on how hopper-like they were. Often, flies cautiously drifted over the trout were ignored, but plop a pattern down beside them and they scoffed it. I especially enjoyed the bow-waves that shot out from banks I'd normally ignore. Yes, trout fixated on hoppers are a wonderful thing, and in large part, we had the wind to thank.

The next day we were committed to the highlands, and as if spiteful about our retreat the previous day, the storm increased in strength. Lindsay, whose credentials include coast guard duty in 20-metre Bass Strait seas, estimated the northerly was gusting to 40 knots. The only chance of shelter was the crater-like surrounds of Woods Lake. Shelter is a relative term when the wind is strong enough to create half-metre swell, but the north shore was at least fishable — at first. There were even black spinners waiting patiently behind rocks and logs, suggesting what might happen if the conditions would abate just a little. Then a cold front shifted the wind from the north to the west and it became difficult to stand up, let alone cast. That was the end of that.

Cruelly, just before the wind change, a couple of duns had emerged and a single large trout had taken my Shaving Brush, which I missed on the strike. I was waiting expectantly for more duns and rises, when the last vestiges of hope disintegrated with the cold front. 'Be nice if the freakin' wind would bugger off now,' I yelled to Lindsay, my patience beginning to fray as we staggered back to the car. I don't think he heard me.

How does that old Chinese saying go? Be careful what you wish for? Under a breathless blue sky at Bronte Lagoon a day later, I was hoping for at least a breeze. The water was so utterly flat that a solitary struggling gum beetle generated ripples which could be noticed from the next bay. We sighted the odd trout, but they were darting around as nervously as a cat at the police dog academy. A few fish actually scared each other, which is never a good sign. The one trout that responded to my Red Tag nosed it and then took off as if it had been scalded.

Then a light easterly sprang up, and everything changed. Suddenly the trout looked like hunters instead of the hunted. Spinners and beetles that had lain safely on the water for hours abruptly began disappearing in sucking rises. The breeze grew stronger until the water was creased by wavelets. I overcast to one memorable trout because it was coming towards me so aggressively. I stripped the Shaving Brush back as fast as I could, yet barely managed to get the fly in front of the fish before I ran out of line. The trout casually took it at the rod tip — I might as well have been made of vapour. Such magnificent moments were commonplace over the next few hours, and Lindsay and I eventually retired before the trout did, an all too rare event.

I awoke the next morning to see the branches swaying gently against a cloudless sky. Beauty, I thought, another perfect polaroiding day. 'Nice little wind Lindsay,' I ventured as he passed the toast.

'Oh, we don't want it just yet,' he replied with a slight frown. 'I'd planned to hit the caenid feeders.'

Lindsay took me to his secret caenid spot anyway. Sure enough, the little mayfly danced by the hundred in the shelter of the forest. But frail as snowflakes, they wouldn't come out on the water while the breeze blew. At the last moment, when the hatch appeared doomed to failure, the wind died away. It seemed only seconds before the noise of rustling gum leaves was replaced by the clips of sipping trout. Yet several good fish later, as the sun rose higher and the caenids faded, my thoughts turned again to polaroiding, and how a bit of wind wouldn't go astray. Lindsay sensed my dilemma as he walked past. 'Let the wind be your friend, Grasshopper,' he said, mimicking the venerable but confusing blind priest from *Kung Fu*.

I laughed but, like Grasshopper, I wasn't entirely sure if I understood.

SUMMER AND SNAKES

MOST OF THE time, and in most respects, I fit right into the standard flyfisher mould. I like that. There is something very reassuring about knowing I share some fundamental sentiments with thousands, possibly millions, of flyfishers worldwide.

The night before a trip, anticipation brings a fitful sleep. I pack with a mixture of excitement and just a dash of anxiety that I will leave something crucial behind. I hope for dry-fly fishing — or, best of all, sight fishing. But I will cheerfully fling a huge wet into a howling gale if that is what's needed. I will feel elated if I land a big one and crushed if I lose it (unless I've caught a few other big ones first). I will enjoy the challenge of a couple of fish beaten on a tough day but also wish for some not-so-tough days! And at least a part of the enjoyment of the trip will be the company of my fishing mates, who I hope will neither do a heck of a lot better than me nor a heck of a lot worse.

But there is one idiosyncrasy I share with no other flyfisher I have ever met, and which brands me in a small but strangely unsettling way as 'different'. I'm not afraid of snakes. I don't mean 'I'm no longer scared of snakes' or 'I'm not too scared of snakes.' I mean I'm as frightened of a snake as you are of a cat. Intellectually, I know a snake can bite me, and this would be a bad thing. If I tread on one, I might get a surprise, but no more so than if I trod on a rabbit. This alone separates me — and by a great distance — from fishing friends who have trodden on snakes and who, ten years later, have never really got over it. Overall, my indifference to snakes excludes me from entire campfire conversations, Internet chat-room discussions, and snake-related talk on where to fish — or, more likely, where *not* to fish.

Now I don't want you to think that my lack of concern towards snakes translates into a general fearlessness towards all the animals a flyfisher might encounter. I'm deeply suspicious of bulls, intensely dislike spiders (especially when I feel them before I see them), and I'm plain scared — like squealing little girl scared — of wasps.

However, I remain unmoved by snakes, and I can never remember it being any other way. In fact, as a six-year-old, my great wish (other than to catch a 3-pound trout like local icon Fred Fry) was to have a pet snake. To my youthful astonishment, it only took a couple of years of Bart Simpson-like nagging for Mum and Dad to relent and buy me a 1.5-metre diamond python. I christened him Percy, and I still think he was the best pet I ever had (apologies to our Labrador Badger — you are *definitely* the uncontested number two).

Percy was such an entertaining pet that I scarcely know where to start. He ate dead mice, which he snatched with slingshot speed and accuracy as they dangled from my fingertips. The ingenuity and near disasters that revolved around maintaining Percy's food supply between mouse plagues and pandemics is a story in itself.

Then there was the time he escaped from his luxurious, electric-blanket-heated quarters and headed straight for the neighbour's duck pen. Any protestations of innocence that Percy might have made the next day were undone by the perfect duckling shape midway down his body. It was something straight out of a Bugs Bunny cartoon, and provided me with possibly my most compelling ever 'Show and Tell'.

But in case you're starting to form a mental picture of a weird little kid not unlike Pugsley from the Addams family, I can truthfully report that Percy also provided plenty of more wholesome, if not entirely conventional, fun. He was an absolute hit at the Mansfield Fete, where annually he would raise a small fortune in the 'Guess the Length of the Snake' competition. On the monkey bars, he was in a class of his own. And it was kind of fun to feel the power as he playfully (I think) constricted on your arm or leg, just as he would in the wild to kill prey. Whoops — beginning to sound like Pugsley again.

Best of all, Percy was often allowed to roam the house during warm weather. We usually remembered to warn visitors, but occasionally we forgot. Honest. I remember watching with fascination as one of the district's toughest cattlemen sipped his tea on the sofa, only to have Percy quietly appear over his shoulder. This bloke was famous for the time he continued to build a fence after a chainsaw blade detached and buried itself in his shoulder. But when Percy's curious tongue tickled his cheek, he jumped like a startled hare and sent tea and biscuits flying.

In hindsight, I suspect more than one of our neighbours thought it just wasn't natural to keep a snake as a pet. But when serious illness struck Percy, there was only bad luck to blame. A blown fuse shut off his electric blanket on a cold night, and by the time Dad noticed, Percy was nearly dead from pneumonia. After a mercy dash to Mansfield, the local vet took a stab (literally) on where to inject antibiotics. The treatment was so successful that within hours Dad reported that Percy was 'chasing the nurses around the waiting room'. Percy went on to make headlines in the *Australian Herpetological Society News* as the first reptile ever treated with tetramyacin. The message is clear: if you ever find a chesty crocodile, goanna or taipan, get some tetramyacin into it as quickly as possible.

The Percy stories go on; suffice to say that if I felt any vestige of fear towards snakes before him, there was none left afterward. And so to this day, as a flyfisher I find myself continually fishing with people who have a phobia I can't relate to. There was Alistair, a great fishing mate for years. Call me thick, but I really did assume that his love of winter fishing was driven by a fondness for smelters and bracing weather. Only some time after he moved interstate did a mutual friend point out that Alistair never went trout fishing after the first warm day of spring because of a chronic snake phobia. Not once.

Then there was the ex-rugby champion I guided. He was about 10 metres away when I failed to notice a copperhead squirming under my boot. My client noticed however. There was subsequent agreement by the others in the party that he did enough running and screaming for both of us.

There are some upsides to being snake-fear free, mostly to do with having whole stretches of rumoured-to-be-snaky lake shore or river to myself. The funny thing is that snake-fearing flyfishers almost seem to want to out-do each other when it comes to describing water as the most snake infested. Last season, I swear that one friend actually managed to scare *himself* out of returning to a stretch of the Delegate River in eastern Victoria, which he had earlier heard was riddled with snakes. In the event, during his adventure my friend caught plenty of trout and didn't see a single serpent. BUT he did *hear* something rustling in the grass. With each re-telling of his Delegate trip, there seemed ever more certainty the rustling sound was made by several giant tiger snakes. A return visit was ruled out.

Yes, having the odd bit of snaky water to myself is okay, but a natural disregard for snakes ultimately leaves me feeling ostracised. This is brought home with special poignancy when I'm excluded from the snake-free bliss that New Zealand apparently brings to normal flyfishers. I can only look on bemusedly at the unabashed joy of my travelling companions as they bound like liberated prisoners through the tussocks and bush. 'But what about the wasps?' I call after them as they disappear into the distance.

COD

THERE'S NOTHING LIKE targeting a new species in the company of an expert to take you back (at least part of the way) to what it feels like to be a novice. All guides should try this from time to time as a reminder of how flyfishing can appear from the opposite side of experience. Apart from the practical value of learning plenty of useful information from which you are likely to benefit for years afterwards, reverting to being the junior member for a change is quite enjoyable. You follow the expert with cheerful faith. They know what's going on and you really don't. This makes it easy to avoid second-guessing. Just sit back and follow the instructions.

When Rob Meade and I finally arranged a day together to chase Murray cod, it was clear from the outset who was the senior partner. What I knew about flyfishing for Murray cod was what I had read — and there is precious little to read. In fact, as I drove across the open plains between my place and the Victorian lake where I'd meet Rob, it occurred to me that a good deal of what I'd read was written by him.

Rob, on the other hand, owes much of his cod knowledge to years spent fishing for them. While he's too canny not to seek information from fisheries scientists and other skilled anglers when he can get it, Rob learns most from his hours on the water.

After a long drive we arrived at the lake around midday. For a change the conditions were perfect, or at least that was Rob's sense of them. Even to a cod novice like me, the overcast sky, humid late-summer warmth and faint breeze felt promising. From what little I knew of cod, the lake itself looked good too. About half of it consisted of open water lined with bulrushes, which terminated at one end in a shallow bowl fringed with short grass. I automatically assessed this area as good water for tailing trout, but any trout that might once have lived in the lake had been eaten by the cod long ago.

The other half of the lake merged into a drowned forest, a grid of rotting spikes like the remnants of an abandoned fort. The trunks became progressively denser the further into the old forest you looked, to the point where it appeared to become impassable to boats. In fact, as I found out later, there were narrow channels where we could sneak around in Rob's 12-foot fibreglass punt.

We rigged up at the launch point as if preparing for tropical game fish, not a southern freshwater species. Our rods were 9-weights, the terminal tackle level 40-pound leaders ending in a 60-pound shock tippet. The flies we tied on of Rob's design were as big and bulky as I'd seen anywhere, collections of fur and feather that could hide my outstretched hand. They had names like Huntsman and Jester and I was reminded that we were fishing for a predator that would tackle astonishingly big prey.

I was acutely aware of this particular aspect of cod behaviour because it so happened that just weeks before I had been talking to Neil Hyatt, manager of fish production at the government hatchery at Snobs Creek, about their Murray cod breeding program. Neil had described absently watching an ibis — a bird about 80 centimetres tall — feeding on the edge of the cod broodstock pond. Neil said he turned away to adjust a valve, heard a large splash, then glanced back to see nothing but a few fluttering feathers. With no sign of a struggle, Neil assumed the ibis had made a narrow escape and flown away. However, when he was checking a couple of anaethetised metre-long cod for eggs a week or two later, one had ibis feet sticking out of its throat.

I told that story to Rob. 'Sounds about right,' he nodded, then gestured at the lake. 'Notice the lack of small water birds like dabchicks and moorhens? Well, in a few months time when the water cools and the cod slow down, they'll come back.' He fiddled with the battery terminals attached to the electric motor. 'But then, when the water warms up again in spring and the cod become active, the birds disappear. I doubt it's a coincidence.'

'So how big do the cod grow here?' I asked Rob as we double-checked our knots and loaded the rods and sandwiches into the boat.

'Not sure,' Rob replied as he pushed us away from the short jetty, 'but we've found rings of tooth marks around the necks of 12-kilogram fish.'

Well, whatever the cod were eating that day it wasn't waterfowl off the top. With no surface activity to speak of we started by searching the areas Rob knew as likely cod lies. By day, cod tend to be ambush feeders, lurking near cover like logs, weedbeds and drop-offs, waiting for prey to swim past. Some of the better snags were invisible and could only be located thanks to Rob's long experience fishing the lake. It took faith to keep putting out casts at invisible structures, letting the fly settle down out of sight and pulling it back.

The first bump was unmistakably a fish, too sharp to be the fly knocking a log or rock. A few casts later, another take was confirmed when a large green shape boiled under the fly just as I lifted off to re-cast. However it was another half hour before I finally strip-striked into a fish and it stayed on. My first-ever cod was a handsome, mottled dark-green fish of about 2 kilograms. It was yet to develop the barrel-like profile that characterises larger cod and it was easily recognisable as belonging to the same family as bass and golden perch. In one sense my cod was an impressive fish to catch on a fly rod, but in another sense it was just a baby.

The afternoon produced more action from 'small' cod up to 3 kilograms or so, interspersed by an occasional yank on the line or bow-wave that appeared to belong to something much bigger. It was all a lot of fun, but I could tell from Rob's general attitude and occasional glance at his watch that we were really only killing time until the main event.

As purple and orange highlights started to appear on the edge of the drab sky, Rob powered up the electric motor, and we glided quietly into the shallow bay at the top of the lake. We changed to floating lines and flies that swam on or just under the surface. Rob inched toward a solitary tussock island and we started casting. After a few strips, a surge of water appeared about where Rob's fly would have been, and an instant later his rod tip lunged down under the weight of a good fish. Rob tightened the drag almost to locked, but the unseen cod simply towed the heavy glass boat in the direction it wanted to go, straight for a tangle of thick weed. Reversing the electric motor, Rob leaned the 9-weight sideways, and the line arced across and then slowly away from the weed fortress. The cod lunged, splashed and rolled after that, but it couldn't repeat the enormous power of its initial run. Gradually Rob coaxed it closer, until at last 10 kilograms of cod slid into his oversized landing net.

This cod was a different animal to the younger models we'd caught up until then: bucket mouth, crocodilian stare, and a body verging on obese. You couldn't call it a pretty fish, but it was impressive. Yet even the dimensions of this cod were soon put in perspective. 'Have a look at this,' said Rob, shaking his head and pointing to the cod's shoulders. A ragged, half-healed scar completely encircled it like a collar. I looked at the white marks and tried to imagine a freshwater fish large enough to attempt to eat a cod the diameter of a dinner plate.

The light was fading rapidly now and we drifted closer to the extreme shallows where the water was no more than knee deep. Even in the twilight it seemed an exposed place to find fish as cryptic as big cod. Yet just as I had that thought, a slow bow-wave disturbed the glassy bay. I led it by a few feet, then gave my Huntsman fly a solid pull. There was an eruption beneath the fly unlike anything I've ever seen a fish generate, a great heaving mass of water like the crest of a deep explosion. I braced for a strike that would pull me from the boat. It never came. Had the fish missed the fly or consciously rejected it? I sat down, shaking and cursing.

By now only the faintest tinge of light still glowed in the western sky. From far across the lake we began to hear metallic clopping sounds. 'Like a bat hitting a baseball isn't it?' said Rob. 'The mudeyes are beginning to migrate across the surface, and the cod are eating them.'

As if to confirm his explanation, a single bug-eyed larva crawled clumsily over the side of the boat to safety. Here, if we didn't disturb it, the mudeye would spend all night growing two pairs of long, elaborate wings. Then it would take flight in the morning sun as a fully formed dragonfly.

There was that sound again, nearer this time. Rob steered the boat towards a pile of logs that emerged from the water close to shore. We both cast toward the logs, but once again it was Rob who came up tight on a fish. 'Bigger I reckon,' he grunted.

This time I couldn't see what was going on very well. It was more a struggle conveyed by sounds. Sharp chirps of drag, pinging line, loud sloshes, and Rob's muttered commentary, half to himself. Eventually I shone the torch on a shape beside the boat that was longer than my arm and many times thicker. The fish weighed 15 kilograms or, for those of us who understand weight better in imperial measurement, about 34 pounds.

It was becoming plain that the nightshift had really begun, and that if we kept fishing on into the dark, encounters with other large cod would be likely. I thought about the bite mark on the 10-kilogram fish Rob had caught earlier with a mixture of excitement and apprehension. In any case it was academic. We both had to be home that evening, and it was time to leave. Back at the jetty, we washed our coffee cups by torch light and a little cod, no more than a pound, appeared in the beam. We noticed how it sensibly hugged the edge of the lake as it raced for caddis and mudeyes, never venturing out beyond ankle depth. 'Smart fish,' said Rob. 'Maybe it'll live to be a 60-pounder.'

Lost in Translation

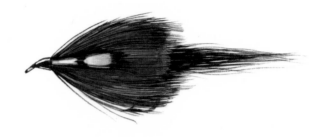

As Peter Julian told it, he was fishing a New Zealand lake late one summer night, alone. The wavelets lapped on the gravel beach behind him under a clear night sky.

Suddenly a heavy fish wrenched the rod tip down. The peace was instantly shattered by the grating whirr of Peter's old reel and the crashing leaps of a big trout, barely visible in the gloom. Then just as Peter was coming to grips with this surprise, there was another. Out of nowhere came a voice: 'Are ya glowin' mate?'

Peter wasn't sure if he was more bewildered by the sudden presence of another person or the unusual and abruptly personal question. Was he *glowing*? Well, it felt good to be fighting a large fish, but 'glowin'' was not how he would have described his present state of mind. While Peter simultaneously wrestled with the trout and an appropriate answer, the stranger piped up again. 'Did ya get 'im on one of those glow flies mate?'

At once it made sense. Peter vaguely recalled a fishing magazine reference to the luminous patterns favoured for night fishing in New

Zealand. He was able to answer the stranger without diverging into a very confused conversation.

Specialist fields develop their own language, at once streamlining exchanges between those in the know and excluding everyone else. In Peter's case, flyfishing-ese comes naturally after several decades spent waving the long rod, but he says that the 'glowin'' exchange taught him that true fluency may never be achieved.

Frequent dealings with novice flyfishers (not to mention non-flyfishing editors) have helped remind me of the obscurity of fly-speak. A tippet is not, in fact, a small additional payment a client offers a barely adequate guide. You do not climb a rise and sheep need not fear a Woolly Bugger.

Even an educated guess isn't enough when trying to understand flyfishing terminology. A dry fly is not actually dry, and there's nothing canine about either the materials or the appearance of a Royal Wulff. When your mate points at the water and says 'shucks', he's not about to be modest.

A charitable person might argue that none of the above names and words was *deliberately* designed to confuse. But even the most generous defender of flyfishing language will struggle to explain away the X system. Sometimes, when I'm taking a flyfishing class, I try to ignore it. But inevitably, I'll notice a bright-eyed beginner staring at their leader packet or tippet spool as if they've found a previously undiscovered Egyptian hieroglyph. 'Hey Phil,' they'll say without looking up, 'what does 5X mean?' The tempting answers are 'Nothing' or 'A lifetime of confusion', and there's truth in both. But in an effort — quite possibly a misguided effort — not to make things more obscure than they already are, I'll usually try to venture an explanation.

For those of you who have blessedly managed to avoid the X topic so far, the simplest way to describe it is that 'number-X' supposedly describes the diameter of tippet material, whether at the business end of a leader or on a separate spool.

But things go downhill from there. For a start, the X system is backwards, so that 1X is many times *thicker* than 7X. This is due to a system that subtracts diameter, in fractions of an inch, from the number 11 (got that?) for reasons too obscure to waste ink here. Given that most of us think about tippet first in terms of breaking strain, this backwards system is a disaster. I am forever dealing with flyfishers — even experienced flyfishers — who, having been asked to bring leaders with decent tippets, proudly brandish their new 6X model. 'That should stop the big'uns!' they say, blissfully unaware they are proposing to fish tippet with the breaking strain of overcooked spaghetti.

I can only talk in vague terms here about breaking strain, because X refers to tippet diameter, not breaking strain, and although the two are related, there is considerable variation depending upon brand and material. You will struggle to land a sick mullet on 6X, but how hard you struggle will vary. 'Okay,' I hear you say in an even voice after a few moments contemplation, 'so X tells us the *diameter*, not the breaking strain.'

Well, yes and no. Some manufacturers can be, shall we say, imprecise when it comes to actual microns of diameter and the X-rating, so that one company's 4X is a different diameter to another company's 4X.

Your smile's starting to look a little stiff by now, but using up the last vestiges of an angler's considerable well of patience, you ask, 'So does the X system offer any advantages at all?'

Well, there is the Law of Four, I concede. This suggests that a given fly-hook size divided by four will give you the appropriate 'X' of tippet to use; i.e. a size 12 fly is best fished on 3X tippet. Except this doesn't really work either. Fly design, variability in hook shape, the weight and power of fish to be landed and whether you want your tippet to assist the fly to float or sink — these points and more all corrupt the original logic so much it barely limps over the line as a vague suggestion, never mind a 'law'.

There is a possible upside to all this flyfishing gobbledygook. It can be used to salvage some pride (revenge?) when conversing with a specialist in a different field. And is there any more worthy target than a computer expert? Up for a summer afternoon's introduction to flyfishing, he was in the middle of telling me how many gigawatts of meglamonics his hard-drive had, when the phone rang. It was my colleague Dasher, seeking the latest update on one of the nearby lakes. 'Well, Dash,' I offered, 'there've been some browns and the odd 'bow smelting along the drop-offs in the afternoon — mainly hitting galaxia pin fry. A size 10 Tom Jones on a figure 8 retrieve's been good, but use 6-pound fluorocarbon tippet.' I paused for breath. 'Then there's the chironomid feeders on evening,' I continued. 'Use 5X mono, and a Milly under a Shaving Brush.' Dash thanked me quickly and hung up — apparently a fish had moved in front of him.

I turned back to the computer whiz, who was looking at me wide-eyed. (I admit I didn't make any effort to keep the phone call quiet.) 'Jeez, this flyfishing sounds complicated,' he exclaimed.

'Oh, the first ten years are the hardest,' I reassured him as we wandered along the lakeshore. 'After that it starts getting easier.'

The next morning I was getting ready to meet some of my favourite guests, a group of electricians who manage somehow to not only work together but enjoy fishing together too. I've been guiding the sparkies for years. These guys are big, capable men — a couple of them are ex-national league footballers. They're so capable in fact, that at times I'm at a loss to know exactly what professional help I can offer other than jogging over to net their next trout.

In any case, as I helped my four-year-old Daniel finish his porridge, he asked 'What are you doing today, Daddy?' Despite having watched me at my lakeside workplace many times, Daniel doesn't quite get the guiding thing yet. I think he struggles with the distinction between Daddy going fishing with friends, and doing it for a living — understandable given I sometimes struggle with the distinction myself. Anyway, this particular morning I was in a hurry, and I simply replied, 'Looking after the sparkies, sweetie.'

Only the previous evening I'd comforted Daniel through a particularly gripping scene in *Toy Story*, and now, as he chewed thoughtfully on his porridge, understanding and sympathy spread across his little face. 'Yes, you're looking after them because they're a little bit scared.'

AUTUMN

LOST AND FOUND

THE TRACK MET the upper South Esk River in Tasmania at a steep rapid. The rocky run above looked good, but the long, languid pool below looked better — especially with two trout sipping in the tail. My friend Neil and I agreed that it was worth a short detour downstream before fishing up as originally planned.

The decision meant a 200-metre walk through the trackless rainforest on the left bank. The autumn sun was just passing over the top of the tall beech trees lining the track, but it was dark and cool the moment we stepped into the bush. I vaguely remember lifting my polaroids onto my cap to see better.

The going wasn't too bad, with the canopy restricting the undergrowth to knee-high ferns. However the obligatory logs — some sound and some rotten — prevented a carefree stride. At one point I was walking along the top of a mossy giant when a whole chunk of it crumbled underfoot.

After a few more minutes we broke out onto the gravel bar below the pool tail. At first it seemed we'd made a wise choice. I spotted a trout immediately, on the edge of the rapid right in front of us. It slashed eagerly at a Shaving Brush before darting under the foam. Never mind, there were at least a couple of fish still rising in the pool tail, and as we moved closer, it appeared there were more like three or four.

Neil crept up and cast toward the nearest riser. Most of the line landed on the stones to the right of the tail, then his little Adams plipped softly on the water not a metre to the right of the fish. It was a lovely presentation. By keeping most of the fly line away from the vacuuming current at the tail, he achieved at least a rod length of drag-free drift, and I watched expectantly for the take. But nothing. Even worse, the other rises above abruptly stopped. What the ... ? Neil's approach and cast couldn't have been more discreet but, somehow, we'd put the fish down. I could only think that the trout I'd missed earlier must have been scared up into the tail, where in turn it had startled the others.

A couple more fish were rising further up the pool where the bubble line dawdled along the shaded right bank, but this time we didn't even get within casting range before the rises stopped. I eventually caught one small trout at the base of the rapid at the end of the track, but it wasn't enough to encourage us to continue further upstream.

The trouble (if that's the right word) with Tasmania is that if one piece of water isn't fishing well there are always plenty of others nearby, vying for attention. With the car only a few metres away, it was an easy decision to leave the rainforest for some sunnier water downstream, where perhaps the trout would be looking harder for food than danger.

We'd travelled around 10 kilometres when the road left the shade of the forest and I reached for my polarised sunglasses to combat the glare. At first I felt inside the vest pocket where I normally keep them, but nothing. Hmmm. Then I remembered putting them on my cap at the start of the walk. I reached up ... nothing there either. With growing concern, I began searching the places I pretty much knew they weren't, like the glove box and the back seat. With a sinking feeling, I came to realise that they *had* been on my cap all right, but somewhere along a 200-metre walk through the rainforest, then up 200 metres of river, they'd fallen off. 'Let's go back and look for them,' said Neil brightly.

'What's the point?' I sighed.

You see, I've lost a lot of things when fishing that I stood a much better chance of finding than those glasses, but never did. Just as a sample, there was the last Elks Pheasant Nymph — the only fly that was working one day on New Zealand's Karamea River — which I dropped on a slate-smooth, room-sized slab of bedrock. I spent half an hour fruitlessly crawling around on that rock as if I were looking for a barely concealed seam of gold. Then there was the weigh net that I cheerfully deposited into the upper Murray River. Evidently I'd failed to line up the magnetic catch properly when I slung it onto the back of my vest after landing a nice rainbow. Distracted by another rising fish, it took me a few moments to associate the splash behind me with a slight but sudden reduction in the weight on my shoulders. Not one to give up a brand new $100 accessory without a fight, I searched the riffles and rapids downstream for the best part of an hour before admitting defeat.

Most depressingly in the current context, a year earlier I'd dropped a pair of glasses in the long grass at Millbrook. I'd realised they were gone within minutes, thus narrowing the possible drop zone down to a few square metres. But despite a team search, and the fact that the frames were a fairly garish silver–gold, the glasses were never seen again.

After explaining this sad record to Neil, I forlornly sealed the argument by pointing out that the present missing pair of glasses was a sort of tree-fern brown colour. 'Well, I still reckon we should have a quick look for 'em,' insisted Neil.

Through my self-pity, I had to admire his attitude. It was his fishing time as well as mine that would be cut short to look for my glasses. Neil was definitely the kind of fishing mate who deserved to be humoured. 'Okay,' I shrugged, not wanting to appear any more ungracious.

We drove back to the track and made some sort of attempt to retrace our steps. Shuffling into the rainforest, our quest seemed doubly futile. One stretch of ferns, logs and moss looked the same as the next, so I couldn't even be sure of the route we'd taken previously. And anyway, the glasses were just as likely to be lying on the bottom of the river. Undeterred, Neil searched like a bloodhound. Then he found a log that looked like the one that had given way earlier, and searched harder. Meanwhile I looked half-heartedly while offering the many reasons why my glasses would never be found, and thanks for trying, but we should just give up and go fishing.

I can't actually remember who saw them first — I think it might have been simultaneous — but there they were: my glasses, lying unharmed beneath a fern frond, about 2 metres from the log. I gaped in speechless astonishment. 'I knew we'd find them,' said Neil without fuss, and began striding back to the car.

Soon after that trip, I lost another net on a local lake (is there a pattern emerging here?). I only realised when I was unpacking the car that night, and my first despairing thought was of all the places it *could* be, like somewhere along 20 kilometres of roadside if I'd left it on the roof. But the next morning, remembering Neil, I took a deep breath, drove off towards the lake and decided to start searching. When I arrived, I thought I recognised the spot where I'd landed my last fish. I walked over, felt around in the weed and mud, and there was my net. Maybe lost doesn't mean forever after all.

Salmon and Trout

We were fishing New Zealand's Owen River in the dying days of the season. Or at least Felix, my mate who owned the lodge in the valley, fished with me. Our friend and guide Craig watched and spotted trout for us, unwilling to cast a rod even on his day off. Cloud swirled around the peaks to the north and autumn rain washed through the valley in gentle waves.

Earlier in the morning large browns had been feeding hard as the river level slowly rose, and we'd caught some good fish of 4 pounds or so. Then at some point which was difficult to define, things got harder. The water became murkier and the flow more daunting. We found ourselves walking further between trout and chances.

As we pushed through the dripping manuka scrub on the bank and stepped carefully over mossy boulders, the idle chatter increased in inverse proportion to the fading fishing opportunities. I noticed the subject of past successes beginning to come up — never a good sign in relation to present opportunities, but entertaining nonetheless. Felix and I had some good stories to tell, but we couldn't compete with Craig, who guides or fishes for around 150 days a year.

I'd just scared a trout I'd spotted too late in a swirling backwater when Craig started talking about a couple of remarkable rivers he'd fished earlier in the season. Craig is quietly spoken and not given to embellishment, so it was all the more compelling to hear him describe these remote rivers where trout as long as your arm apparently spent their lives just waiting for the opportunity to wolf down an artificial fly.

Felix and I listened with fascination, not least because the rivers Craig described were ones we'd always assumed fished poorly. I recalled they received only a few unpromising lines in the guidebooks, and during many discussions with other anglers over the years, I'd never heard them mentioned.

As you might expect, talk turned to the possibility of the three of us going there together one day. It would be a fair expedition as these rivers were a long way away: a trip to plan with care when conditions looked perfect, perhaps in mid summer. But as Craig was describing how, just a couple of months earlier, a 12-pounder had pursued a cicada pattern down a rapid, Felix said, 'I want to go there now!' It was an almost childlike comment, a desire expressed that, for all sorts of practical reasons, stood no chance of actually happening. Felix knew it, and added an ironic chuckle.

'Well, it would be possible,' said Craig, joining in the game. 'We'd just have to drive for hours in the dark, cancel tomorrow's commitments, and hope for fine weather.' He pushed a fallen branch to the side of the path. 'And after all that the fishing might be no good anyway. I've never been in there this late in the season.'

Felix paused and looked at both of us with a grin. 'Then how do we know it won't be brilliant?'

So it was that somehow, despite all the good reasons not to go, we found ourselves weaving along dark roads in the wee hours of the following morning. After much discussion, we'd settled on the stream that Craig felt would be holding the bigger trout. It still felt outrageous to be going at all, yet despite the easier and more reliable fishing options we'd left behind, it was hard not to be excited.

Some hours later we were on foot, cresting the ridge at the top of a gorge. The silvery ribbon of the river wound its way into the distance below us and then disappeared into the bony mountains beyond. The sun shone brightly and skylarks flitted between thorny bushes and yellowing tussocks, but the air was crisp and frost crunched underfoot in the shadows of the larger rocks. The river seemed to be at a good level, having obviously escaped the rain system we'd earlier experienced on the Owen. It was very clear with the faintest tinge of blue and looked crossable. As we walked it seemed to me we were bypassing some very nice water, but Craig insisted the best fishing lay further upstream, and Felix and I knew better than to second-guess the master.

Eventually Craig veered down the slope to where the river transcribed an S shape across a small flat at the top of the gorge. Up close it was a large stream, perhaps 20 metres across. Where the clear current constricted into a steep rapid downstream, it appeared powerful and dangerous, but the tail of the glide in front of us looked as if it could be crossed with care.

Felix started fishing first. The morning sun was still too low in the sky to enable good polaroiding, so he began searching the likely seams and bubble lines with a small bead-head Pheasant Tail Nymph, about a metre beneath a yarn indicator. The fly would have fitted comfortably on Felix's thumbnail and seemed too insignificant for a fish to notice. I had to remind myself that in the ice-clear conditions even a tiny nymph would draw the attention of a trout. With their large eyes and broad vision field, big browns are experts at drift feeding as they scan the places where the current lines concentrate for any suspicion of food.

While Felix searched the likely lies, Craig and I carefully viewed the river from higher up. Two-thirds of the way to the top of the glide, Craig stopped and tilted his head from side to side. 'Might have one here, Felix,' he announced matter-of-factly as he usually does. 'Just on the outer edge of that big square rock.'

I stared towards the same submerged boulder, which rose to within half a metre of the surface on the edge of a deep chute. I imagined I saw the faintest dark smudge behind the boulder move out into the current and back again. Felix's first cast was short, but the second seemed perfect, his 4-metre leader unrolling so the nymph plopped gently into the water on a line with the outer edge of the boulder and just upstream of it. The little green yarn indicator was surprisingly visible from our vantage point 30 metres away, and I watched transfixed as it bobbed past the point where I thought I'd seen something. Right then a shape glided out and up, transforming into the distinct shape of a large trout as it rose closer to the surface. As the fish came up higher and higher, I had a moment to appreciate that I'd underestimated the depth of the water, when the trout made a deliberate movement and Craig shouted 'Strike!'

Given that Craig's usually so quiet and understated, hearing him shout 'strike' is like being poked with an electric cattle prod. I think I struck myself, and Felix certainly did. His line jumped from the water and the rod was instantly bowed under the weight of the fish. The trout weaved between boulders, leapt high, then raced down the river. Felix kept up, leaning the rod sideways and only allowing the fish to take a little line. It was a good strategy and the trout turned back upstream well before reaching the point where the river tumbled into the gorge below. Soon Craig had unclipped his landing net and was waiting for Felix to bring the big brown within range. It flew clean out of the water one final time … and the hook pulled out. Just like that. Well, at least we knew there were trout around, and that they could be hooked.

I was up next. Our rules about taking turns to fish can seem ruthless after a loss like that: you get a chance at a fish, and win, lose or refusal it's the next guy's turn. Felix would have to wait to make amends. We walked down to the tail of the glide and crossed to the right side. The glide was wide enough for this side to be undisturbed and further up it settled into a pool of sorts. The riverbed here was made up of small stones and the surface was only faintly disturbed by the current. The angle of the sun was perfect for spotting. We had no trouble sighting the first candidate, finning quietly off the bank about 50 metres up. Even from a distance it was clearly a beauty, and I muttered some calming words to myself as I snuck carefully into position, using the high lip of the bank as cover. I was just stripping off line for a cast when a gigantic shape came tearing down the river and straight past the 8-pounder I was about to cast to. 'What the … ?' was all my bewildered brain could come up with as a fish that looked like a 4-foot trout, but couldn't possibly be, dwarfed my target and sent it fleeing to the undercuts. 'Bugger,' said Craig. 'Salmon.' And so began one of the most surreal flyfishing sessions I've experienced.

Chinook salmon are a part of the South Island fishery that many fly anglers never encounter. The life cycle of chinooks is well known thanks to frequent appearances in wildlife documentaries and *National Geographic*, but it bears repeating. Born in the headwaters of select rivers, the young salmon smolts migrate to the ocean, where they grow at a rate few riverine environments can match. Depending on the number of years at sea, the New Zealand fish return as adults typically weighing between 10 and 40 pounds, sometimes more. Once they re-enter fresh water the salmon cease feeding, relying on their reserves to travel great distances to their spawning grounds.

Famously, all Pacific salmon, including chinooks, are on a death march once they return to their home rivers. The fish undergo chemical and hormonal changes upon entering fresh water that eventually prove lethal. Not only do these changes cause the salmon to stop eating, the fish effectively begin to rot from within — a remarkable if gruesome piece of evolutionary development that ensures their carcasses are immediately available to fertilise the spawning grounds, rather than drifting uselessly downstream. By the time they are actually laying and fertilising their eggs in the gravel, the salmon are virtually bags of mush. At least the kids will have plenty to eat.

We began to encounter more and more salmon as we fished upstream. On paper, these fish were the living dead, in their last weeks or even days before spawning and perishing. But as they shot up rapids like missiles, bow-waved through pools and chased each other and the trout with tireless abandon, they didn't look it.

No doubt about it, the salmon were sabotaging fishing opportunities. Typically we would find a trout and sneak up for a cast, only to have a salmon come screaming out of nowhere. Even those salmon that didn't actually chase the trout probably unnerved them. I imagined a 10-pound trout watching a 20-pound chinook zoom past, and thinking, 'What the heck scared *that*?'

There were countless memorable moments. On one occasion we found an apparently active trout in the very tail of a long glide, right where the bubble line flowed out. I cast to the monster with shaking hands, covering it perfectly with a Shaving Brush dry. But something wasn't right. It dropped back further and further into the ankle-deep riffle edge I was standing in, its tail and dorsal emerging as it became shallower. Craig peered over the high bank above and saw that a huge chinook was prowling the pool tail. The trout I was casting to wasn't feeding, it was trying to hide!

Then there was the beauty rising steadily in a long pool for the first duns of the day — a sitter for Felix surely. But even before he reached position, a team of bow-waves sped through the pool. After the combined wakes died away the duns were still drifting down but the rises had stopped.

The salmon didn't sabotage all our chances. Craig found two trout feeding quite well in a run at the top of a gorge, which he pointed out to me from a knoll 30 metres above the stream. The slope down to the river here was so steep that only a good cover of brush made it safe to descend. I made my way down, zigzagging from bush to bush. I reached the riverbank and carefully peered over the edge, only to spook a third trout we hadn't noticed. It sped up the river and frightened the other two. Arrghh!

Above the gorge a very long if quite shallow pool beckoned. Whether it was the lack of depth or the lack of structures like logs and boulders, the pool seemed miraculously devoid of salmon. But not trout. At the same moment, Craig and I picked up the shape of a cruising trout, wandering upstream and away in the gentle current, then turning and approaching us. In a few seconds it was nearly upon us and I barely had time to drop to my knees and flick out a short cast. The nymph settled beneath the indicator, the fish deviated slightly, opened its mouth, and I lifted. A 7-pound brown tore across the broad turquoise flats of the pool, trailing a plume of silt and my line. The many subsequent runs were long and spectacular but the trout had nowhere to go — no nearby rapids to charge down, no rocks or logs to burrow beneath. With the sort of nervous patience that comes with hooking a fish after many missed shots, I gradually worked the trout closer until it was shaking its head back and forth beside the bank. It was an easy net shot for Craig and he didn't miss. I flopped back theatrically on the frost-burned grass and sighed with relief and delight.

That pool and that fish proved a rare interlude from the salmon. As the April sun finally generated some afternoon warmth, duns began drifting down the next pool in the largest numbers we'd seen all day. A trout rose twice and Felix raced into position, but two huge salmon bow-waved down and the rises stopped. The story was repeated throughout the afternoon: duns, some rises, and then big salmon tearing around ruining it all. We tried to get angry about it, but the salmon were too spectacular.

At last Craig found a trout rising in an undisturbed backwater, a brown so big that he actually mistook it for a salmon until it sipped down a dun as he peered over the bank (the salmon don't feed). While I waited at a safe distance, Felix and Craig knelt on the high bank above the backwater. Craig's normally cool commentary was sharp and breathless, and it was clear the trout was huge. The main action was hidden from me by the lip of the bank, but it seemed one of Felix's flicked casts finally drew a take. Alas, there was no hook-up, and soon after the giant trout just melted away.

The next pool beckoned of course, and the next. In fact, the river seemed to only get better as it snaked its way across a floodplain that broadened briefly before another gorge. But already the shadows of the peaks to the west were creeping towards us, swallowing first the river edges and then whole bends. I walked upstream and into the shade, hoping to find one more riser to cast to. It was like walking into a cold room. Just a few metres behind, the river looked alive and the duns danced, but here in the gloom winter waited. My breath fogged and my fingertips grew numb. The river here was grey and cold, a place for dying salmon and new eggs perhaps, but not dry flies and duns. Craig called out from downstream with Felix winding in beside him. 'Better get going Phil, it'll be dark in an hour.' I took a last long, hard look at the river, then turned and began walking toward the pink streaks of sunlight on the hillside.

LUCKY

NICK WAS A quietly spoken country GP who single-handedly looked after a town of a couple of thousand. After almost a year without a break, he'd managed to steal a few autumn days flyfishing down my way.

Nick insisted from the start that simply being out fishing was enough, and any trout caught would be a bonus. I summoned a mental image of his waiting room during 'flu season, and grasped his point. However, I also thought if anyone deserved to catch some trout, it was Nick.

On my wish-list of supernatural fishing powers, right after being able to see the trout with some sort of miraculous infrared vision, comes a desire to allocate fishing luck based on merit. For example, I'd serve a decent helping to the fifteen-year-old who's saved for six months for his day out, while perhaps being less generous to the dour tourist who exclaims after a few pitiful casts, 'When am I going to catch a fish?' The reality is, of course, that the deserving still miss out sometimes, while the wastrels (and isn't that a perfect word) occasionally enjoy success to which they have dubious entitlement.

But whether Nick's fortunes were beyond my powers or not, I certainly hoped things would go his way. As it turned out, for the next day and a half, his luck ran at about half pace. That is, he didn't suffer any of the real tragedies of fishing — no trout were lost just as the landing net was drawn, nor did his rod snap mid-cast while presenting the fly to a once-a-year trophy. On the other hand, the weather was cold and grey. There were also a few times I could have sworn he struck perfectly but the trout swam off safely. Nevertheless, Nick seemed happy in his own quiet way, insisting with each trout actually landed that his expectations were being exceeded.

By lunch on the last afternoon, Nick's attitude was rubbing off on me. Following a restorative hot meal, we strode off along the lakeshore in good spirits. I philosophically noted to myself that, although Nick had been cheated following a couple of strong chances, he'd also landed several nice trout. As for the weather, at least it hadn't actually rained.

We were passing a thick clump of bulrushes when, despite the poor light, I spotted a large rainbow — 5 pounds at least — cruising into the cove ahead. I'd rigged Nick with a perfect setup for autumn sight fishing: an indicator with a stick caddis 30 centimetres below on a dropper, with a superglue buzzer a further 30 centimetres below on the point. In an excited whisper, I directed Nick to the fish, whose fuzzy shape now circled out and back towards the bulrushes. It's always risky to cast after a departing trout, so we took a gamble it would come back and offer a better shot. A minute or so later, the big rainbow reappeared, right on the same beat into the cove. Nick's short cast was fast and accurate, leading the fish by about 2 metres. Perfect! Sure enough, the fish began to accelerate in the direction of the flies ... but then, with the 5-pounder still a metre short, the indicator dived. What the ... ?

Instinctively, Nick lifted. The rod tip buckled, and a previously unseen 3-pounder leapt clear of the water, red superglue buzzer clearly visible in its top lip. There was hardly time to comprehend, but I had just a moment to think 'Oh no!' as the smaller fish belly-whacked right on top of the big one. The larger rainbow instantly fled. 'Ah well,' said Nick, smiling, 'a fish in the hand ...'

'Yeah, sure,' I nodded, trying to sound upbeat. 'And that's still a good fish.' I didn't add we'd caught 3-pounders already, but not a 5-pounder.

The young rainbow fought hard, tearing right, then left and leaping again. But wait a second ... Young rainbow? Suddenly it looked bigger, more like the 5-pounder again. Had our eyes fooled us? No, there was an explanation. Instead of being terrified by the commotion, the bigger trout had reappeared and was now shadowing the smaller fish, perhaps indignant at the intrusion into its territory.

Then the unusual changed to the incredible. The larger rainbow suddenly spotted the stick caddis racing along just in front of the intruder. Apparently, its pea-sized brain didn't get as far as questioning how a sluggish stick caddis could do 5 knots: another fish was trying to eat *its* food, and that wasn't on. With an extra beat of its tail, the bigger trout shot to the front, and seized the stick caddis.

Now, let's draw breath for a moment and contemplate what happens when a 3-pounder and a 5-pounder find themselves on the same line. It sounds like every angler's dream, but think about it. What's the physical equation when two decent trout swim hard in the opposite direction — as they inevitably will — while tethered by a single length of flyfishing tippet? The angler can play the trout as carefully as possible, but it won't matter: a double bust-off is the only possibility.

Or is it? I've made many mistakes in my fishing life, and no doubt more lie ahead. But one thing I've learned from bitter experience is to *always* tie the point fly on slightly weaker tippet than the dropper fly. Not in case of a double hook-up (a once-in-a-blue-moon event), but because whenever a fish is hooked on the dropper, the point fly then trails dangerously behind, easily snagging on any obstruction.

Blessedly, this 'rule' has become second nature to me, and I'd applied it subconsciously when tying Nick's rig. It remained inevitable that *a* trout would break off, but hopefully only the one on the point.

In a few seconds, the surreal 'baton change' happened, virtually seamless. First there was one trout on the line, then briefly two, then one again — only it had nearly doubled in weight! An angler fishing alone and not paying close attention might have wondered if he'd been out too long in the country air.

Of course the big trout was completely fresh when it took over and poor Nick basically had to resume the original struggle from scratch. But he was up to the challenge, and when he began to complain about his tired rod arm, he didn't actually look too upset. After a few more minutes, I had a chance with the net, the trout slid in, and that was that. Luck had well and truly gone Nick's way and, I thought silently, rightly so.

Many months have passed since that remarkable day, but I like to think that when Nick's waiting room gets too crowded or he has to make a midnight house call, he remembers the 5-pounder and how fortune does, in fact, go the right way sometimes.

THE CREEK

FISHING HAS ALWAYS had an ambiguous relationship with time. Most anglers know the old adage that the hours spent fishing are added to your allotted lifespan, not subtracted from it. Then there are periods when time can't pass fast enough, like when there are weeks or — heaven forbid — months between you and the next big fishing trip. On the other hand, the trip itself often passes too quickly.

Occasionally, time marches on in a way that's cause, if not for melancholy, then contemplation. The other day I stopped in at a creek I've fished a few times a season for twenty years or more except, on this occasion, two years had slipped by since my last visit.

I usually fish the creek on Jack's place. I only know him by his first name, but most visits to the creek begin by calling in at Jack's basic farmhouse amid a cacophony of barking dogs. Although I can't wait to start fishing, I never begrudge the unrushed chats with Jack before I drive across the paddock and down to the creek. Partly that's because, while not an angler, Jack always has some fascinating insight to offer about what's been happening on the creek that in turn relates to the fishing. He might tell me about the size and duration of the last flood, how the creek survived the fires, or even how 'There's been a lot of them little white moths down the pump hole on evening, and fish jumpin' too.' But talking with Jack is also interesting simply for the insights into a very different life to mine, and sometimes for the wisdom he unintentionally offers.

This time, when he opened the front door there was a flicker of hesitation, possibly as he tried to recall my name after a two-year absence. Perhaps I hesitated too, for it struck me how much Jack had aged. Visits to the creek had always had a timelessness to them, something that was remarkably reassuring, and Jack was part of that. But after a two-season break, there was no disguising the fact that he was no longer the wiry, energetic man of the land I had first met all those years ago. It crossed my mind that I might knock on Jack's door one day and find he wasn't there anymore.

And so I fished the rest of that day in a reflective frame of mind. Not too reflective of course. Every autumn rainbow that seized the Royal Humpy or Wulff brought me smartly back to the here and now. Then there was one big brown that sauntered up under a Keam hopper and followed it at nose distance halfway down the run. I spent the next quarter-hour changing flies and drifts, and thinking of nothing else but how to catch that trout. But in between, I thought a lot about the passage of time. The creek itself was comfortingly familiar. The fish were pretty much there in the same numbers and size as always. True, some years they had averaged a little heavier, other years a little lighter. But a 10-incher was standard, a pounder cause for a satisfied grunt, a solitary 2-pounder reason for a chuckle out loud that would have alarmed any passer-by. And had I hooked the 3-pounder, this story wouldn't have been about anything else.

The same flies that had worked twenty years ago were (more-or-less) working now. Humpys, Wulffs and hoppers, sometimes with a bead-head nymph beneath. I tried the relatively recent innovation of a little tungsten-beaded pattern at one point, but in the gentle early autumn flow it pulled the dry under too easily, and it kept catching the bottom. I changed back to a plain old brass-beaded version and caught a fish first cast. Sometimes newer doesn't equal better.

For all that was the same, however, some things had changed over the years. The irresistible riffle beside which I once impatiently unpacked a student-era Falcon 500 had long since changed into one of the largest, stillest pools on the stream. The anabranch where I would always split up with my fishing mate (and never quite know who got the better deal until we reached the top) was now a single channel. You had to look very hard at the slight depression beneath a thicket of wattle to know a side-stream ever flowed there.

It occurred to me that sometimes the fishing mate in question was Paul, back then a likely starter for any impromptu trip. Last year when I planned to head up Jack's way with Paul, we put the weekend in the diary five months early and he still had to pull out in the end. At a social gathering recently, a mutual friend spoke admiringly of how successful Paul had become. I nodded, but silently wondered if a 90 per cent reduction in fishing time constituted success.

Paul isn't the only fishing mate whom I see less and less. Photo albums, book pages and old articles have become a chronicle of trips and people past, and here and there are pictures of the creek. On the bright side, there are mates like Felix who didn't even know what a fly rod was fifteen years ago, but who has since sold his business to run a fishing lodge.

It was twilight by the time I approached the pool (previously the riffle) where the farm track met the creek. I could just see my Subaru parked under the weeping willow where the old Falcon, and a few cars in between, had also patiently waited.

The trout were rising in the long, narrow tail. There was no doubt about it, for evening fishing at least, this flat water with a clear western bank was better than the long-gone riffle ever was. I tried to look through the risers to find that one special fish. Almost hidden by a tussock on the far side, I noticed it — quiet sips behind the vigorous rises in the foreground. The cast was perfect and so was the strike ... I thought. There was heavy weight for a moment, heavier than I'd felt all day, before the fly sprang back at me. I didn't mind too much: even hooking a trout like that showed that after two decades I had learned a thing or two about this creek.

Then as I walked back to the car, I wondered. By the trout's standards, I'd been fishing the creek forever, catching fish that were great-great-great-grandchildren of the first I'd hooked. By my own standards, I had clocked some serious miles here. But as far as the creek was concerned, I was a blink in time.

THE LONG MARCH

I SAY THIS respectfully, but my good friend DJ likes his fishing easy. Give the man a mid-autumn dun hatch, a gentle breeze, sun on his back and lots of slightly stupid trout, and you couldn't move him from the water with a winch. However, DJ's response to a lack of action is to select a nice soft tussock out of the wind and take a nap. His solution to fussy trout, no matter how well they're feeding, is to head somewhere else. Cold, wind or rain are all compelling reasons to leave the water at once and find a cosy pub.

But if there's one thing above all others that DJ considers incompatible with a good day's fishing, it's a long walk to get there — or, even worse, a long walk to get back. No matter what angling riches are promised at the end of the trail, my sedentary mate won't go, at least not willingly.

In DJ's own best interests then, it can be necessary to be a little vague about the detail of some routes. 'I thought you said it was downhill all the way,' puffed DJ on a recent trip as we tackled a steep ridge that lay between us and the river.

'Didn't I say *most* of the way?' I queried innocently. 'Anyway,' I added brightly, 'this bit will be downhill on the way back.'

Long walks and flyfishing have a significant association. Everyone believes the further away from the road you go, the better the fishing. This may not always be strictly true but it's a powerful perception. Having fought your way down tangled, giddy slopes (or in some Tasmanian instances, *up* giddy slopes), you at least know that whatever challenges the trout may present, competition from other anglers is unlikely to be an issue. As a bonus, beer cans and other rubbish are absent, because it's a happy fact that the sort of people who litter are invariably repelled by having to travel any distance on foot.

I spend a lot of time fishing a mere stroll from the car or cabin, but every season throws up a few fishing trips where I end up walking a long way. These journeys can take several forms. First, there are those in the 'wonder what's in the next bay?' category. Although these walks may stretch to a few kilometres, they're usually at the tame end of the spectrum. They happen on lakeshores, which tend to offer flat, open walking with expansive views. You can maintain enough perspective on how far you've travelled to avoid any nasty surprises when you head back. At Lake Purrumbete the other day, I did find myself questioning why I'd walked from the south side of the lake to the north side when the former was fishing well, but it's not like I suddenly thought 'How did I come to be so far away?'

Not to be confused with this first type, are the 'wonder what's around the next bend?' ventures while stream fishing. I suspect I'm not alone in saying that if a stream is fishing well, it seems to induce a trance-like, semi-deluded state. Never mind the patently impenetrable scrub on the bank, or the greased-boulder riverbed, you kid yourself that it won't matter if you fish on just a little further. One hour turns to four. Before you know it, you're faced with a trek back downstream to break the stoutest spirit — and possibly an ankle if you're not careful.

On some expeditions the walking begins long before you get to the water. Given that most anglers don't decide to arbitrarily wander off into the bush, in these cases the route has usually been planned, so you have some idea of how far you're going and what you're in for.

Trips you've done before are, of course, the most predictable, but even here you have to be careful. I read once that the human brain has a propensity to remember the good and forget the bad (just ask any old timer how the fishing was when he was a lad). This is something to take into account when heading back to that bottomless gorge which fished so well five years ago. You're mentally hooking those 3-pounders like it was yesterday, but what about that 1000-metre climb out, up a 45-degree slope?

As for treks to new places, I usually contemplate them with a mix of excitement and apprehension. Not long ago I found myself standing at the base of a very steep, 900-metre-high bluff in the Cradle Mountain wilderness. I carried a pack that felt heavy before I'd taken a step, the lake was at the top, and the track went straight up. For a moment I had a crystal-clear view of the world from the DJ perspective. I had driven past plenty of good fishing to get here, so what on earth was I doing?

And then I thought back to another experience. I was fishing the upper Matakitaki River in New Zealand with Craig Simpson on a cool, bright autumn day. My gaze wandered to the stupefyingly high ridge beside us, so steep it appeared as if its 2-kilometre-high crest might topple over. 'Imagine, no one would ever have stood up there,' I murmured, half to myself.

'Actually I have,' said Craig matter-of-factly. 'We hunt chamois up there.'

'How?' I gaped, trying to sound nonchalant myself, but failing dismally.

'Oh we tramp up,' he said, already moving on and looking for the next fish. 'A bit steep when it's wet though.'

Back at the base of the bluff in Tasmania, I drew a deep breath and headed off. Legs are made for walking after all.

ONE LAST CAST

THROUGH MUCH OF Victoria, a hot, dry summer stretched into early autumn, so the abrupt change to rain and cold in April came as a bit of a shock. In the space of a week, I went from wet wading to Gore-Tex, broad-brim to beanie. When our local firewood man came down with the 'flu, I had to fell the dead tree in the front yard to keep us going until he could deliver.

The perceived sharpness of the shift from summer to winter wasn't just a case of us getting soft over the balmy months. To prove we weren't imagining things, April produced three big snowfalls in the Victorian Alps, and even lowly Lake Mountain had a skiable cover for days.

A busy early autumn schedule caused several postponements of a trip to the north-east Victorian rivers. Autumn and north-east fishing trips have been a part of my life since I was six years old, as certain as the leaves turning and the days getting shorter. There was no question I was going; it was just a matter of when.

With the endless warm, settled days in March, it seemed there was no hurry to catch the best of the north-east autumn fishing, and the trips missed or cancelled were of little concern. (Well, except for the 'should've been there' reports from friends who went.) But the unexpected onset of August-like conditions in April suddenly ramped up the urgency. Finally, my old friend Malcolm (who divides his time between the city and his country property) and I managed to find three compatible days and off we went to the Ovens valley and Mal's nearby farm.

The Ovens and its feeders could not have looked lovelier, lined with yellow-gold poplars, flaming oaks and cottonwoods. Even the despised crack willows were briefly beautiful with their sprinkled orange-and-butter leaves. The rivers themselves were low-ish, with the almost brittle clarity you find in the latter half of autumn.

In one sense, we were too late. We drove up under piercing blue sky with the sun hot through the windscreen, but when we walked in the door of Mal's old cottage it was like entering a fridge. The clammy chill and musty smell trapped inside spoke already of long cold nights and frosty dawns. The fire roared in the hearth for an hour before the place felt welcoming.

Sure enough, the rivers were ice cold, just 8 or 9°C. It took a little while before we realised the fishing 'rules' of summer no longer applied. The water was lifeless until 11 a.m., and the coveted evening rise of a month ago had dwindled to a few half-hearted sips that ceased altogether by dark. Even during the best time of 11 'til 5, the swift heads of the pools and the pocket water and riffles between weren't hotspots anymore. Now the trout lazed in bubble lines or even sluggishly cruised the bigger, stiller pools like lake fish. It was as if they were slowly freezing up with the approach of winter — until they were hooked that is!

And hook them we did — plenty — once we worked out what they were doing. It was exacting fishing: quick, accurate casts with long leaders and small dries before we lost sight of the trout or they stopped rising. But Mal and I had had all season to practise and mostly we were up to the challenge.

While repetition might dull some of life's pleasures, it never seems to when fish are taking the dry. I was transfixed by every take. I was often able to watch a trout as it swam over to the tiny fly, considered it for a moment, then sipped it under with barely a ripple. Mal thought I lifted too slowly on some of the fish but I think it was just time standing still.

There's often a particular trout that's more memorable than the others. This one was lying a metre below the surface in a large, round pool, motionless as a river rock, and I almost didn't see it. I flicked the Adams over the fish, and for four or five seconds nothing happened. Then it rose up so slowly that Mal had time to say, 'Would you look at that, I think it's half asleep!' The brownie hesitated under the fly, surely not fooled after such a lengthy inspection? But it was, and it sucked the fly in with conviction. It certainly woke up after that.

The last afternoon we fixed a fence that had copped a tree limb during a storm a week earlier, then headed out for one final go. It was getting late and already the river was enveloped in soft-blue autumn shadows. The trout still rose here and there, but often they were oncers. The fishing was hard now, and when Mal hooked a 1-pound rainbow and brought it to hand there was a definite sense of occasion. Time was running out, and with it, the end of our mountain stream fishing for the season.

We had planned to depart in time to negotiate the narrow road away from the farm in daylight, but just as we started walking up the hillside to the car, another fish rose twice, further up the glide. 'Just one last cast,' I called out to Mal, and scrambled around the bank to get closer. As if on cue, the trout rose again as I made it into position. Even in the poor light I glimpsed it — a bigger fish, maybe 2 pounds. I cast low beneath the tea-tree branches, and the Adams sailed perfectly, landing just up and to one side of the spreading rings. I waited ... waited. Nothing. I cast again, a little further up this time, in case the fish was cruising slowly up the bubble line, but no response.

'We'd better keep moving, Phil,' reminded Mal from the hillside above. I watched for a few more moments, but the trout didn't rise again.

I reeled in with mixed feelings, glad of rising fish and dry-fly fishing on my final mountain stream trip of the season, but sad it was over. Halfway up the hill, I stopped to admire the sweep of the river one more time, and the trout rose again, right where I'd just been standing. 'You bastard!' I chuckled to myself. 'Next season.'

FLYING BLIND

AUTUMN IS A season of transition when it comes to many aspects of flyfishing, and not least when sight fishing for trout. On the one hand, the mild, stable weather that characterises the first part of autumn is a sight-fishing highlight in many places. Along the rivers, insect life — terrestrial and aquatic — is reaching a crescendo. With cooler water temperatures and softer light than high summer, this is one of the best times to find daytime rises on a number of rivers. It doesn't hurt that the trout seem to sense the abundance won't last forever and feed up accordingly.

The lakes and the trout therein follow a similar trend, although the same settled early autumn conditions that unambiguously help river fishing create the calm, bright conditions which can make lake trout easy to spook.

Then, some time in the latter half of autumn, conditions change. The timing varies from place to place and from year to year; however, at a certain point, the dominant high-pressure cells and their stable weather move north, replaced by the frequent passage of strong cold fronts. In weeks, if not days, autumn switches from a memory of summer to a prelude to winter. On the rivers, the peak fishing just described can fade in a matter of days, particularly in the mountains. I've been there for the changeover and no amount of wishing can reverse the trend.

On lakes, the transition isn't as negative. Once you get used to dressing correctly, and you remind yourself that trout are, after all, a cold-water fish, the fishing in late autumn becomes quite enjoyable. However, there's one shift that some people never adjust to, and that's the reduction in sight-fishing opportunities. Note I said reduction, not cessation — there are still plenty of good chances to cast to sighted trout through late autumn and even in winter. Nevertheless, there's no point in denying that these chances are basically reduced. Far fewer insects of interest to trout are active in the cold, so surface feeding is limited. And when the trout aren't on the surface, reduced light makes them harder to see beneath it. Not only are sunny days with good trout-spotting light rarer, when such days do occur the light penetration is less, the shadows are longer and the hours of high sun are fewer. In summary, during mid to late autumn, sight fishing is in decline. It is replaced more and more by searching, where you rely solely on secondary cues to ensure your fly and the invisible fish cross paths.

This kind of fishing is often referred to as blind fishing or, even more severely, as blind *flogging*. Interestingly, among flyfishers, those who dislike blind fishing most passionately tend to be beginners or the very experienced, rather than those in between. Beginners find blind fishing tough because of its subtlety. 'It's hard enough to catch these trout when you can see them!' they say in exasperation. Meanwhile, among those with a decade or more flyfishing behind them, there are some who, by this point in their careers, have enjoyed so much good sight fishing that they simply can't get excited by the idea of doing anything else.

I'll state here without reservation that pretty much the only thing that matters in flyfishing is your enjoyment of it. If you are only happy fishing dry flies, fine. If you like to push the boundaries by, say, casting flies that look suspiciously like soft plastics, that's fine too. The only thing I'd suggest is that people don't confuse their personal aesthetic preferences with how easy or hard, or skilful or not, a particular kind of flyfishing is.

When I travelled to the Snowy Mountains in late May with my fishing mate, artist and colleague Trevor Hawkins, we knew we wouldn't be able to rely on sight fishing. With luck there might be sunny patches around the middle of the day that would permit polaroiding, or a sparse rise for the half-hour around sunset. But for hours, possibly whole days, we would need to search for the trout with our flies, not our eyes.

And that was how it turned out. On the first evening we worked the eastern shore of Lake Jindabyne and a smattering of fish rose despite a cold wind and precious little visible food. It was sight fishing of sorts: the rises were too irregular to offer the chance of covering fish precisely, but the swirls and slashes were still the focus. If you saw a fish rise, you cast a fly to the area as quickly as possible. Although the movement we observed was almost certainly in response to small insects like caddis, midge or craneflies, we judged the hatch too light to go down the imitative path. Instead we used large wet flies, operating on the principle that the trout were unlikely to be committed to selectively targeting the few tiny bits of surface food. Bigger wets, retrieved to cover a decent area of water, were more likely to attract attention. We reasoned that these wets would be recognised as food by fish accustomed to encountering large perennial Jindabyne prey like mudeyes, yabbies and goldfish.

Whatever the thought processes of the trout, the tactic worked and we landed several rainbows to 2 pounds or so: not monsters, but fat, silvery Jindabyne fish that pulled as hard as many trout twice the size.

It was a good start, but the next day was more testing. We drove through an ice-shrouded landscape in the dawn light to Lake Tantangara. The snow gums by the roadside glistened like giant chandeliers, and in the valleys, a freezing mist thwarted the first rays of sun. When we finally arrived at the lake it was as frigid as a tomb.

Still, what was it I said earlier about trout and cold? Even as we rigged up with gloved hands on the frozen lakeside marsh, a fish swirled, then a few minutes later, another. Both trout were too far out to reach, but at least there was activity. Every five minutes or so, another fish would move somewhere. The lake was glassy calm, and we could see every swirl, even those hundreds of metres away. This was great inspiration for the likely blind searching that lay ahead. We couldn't cover these fish in any meaningful sense — they were either too far out to reach or else so distant that, by the time we reached the spot, the fish could have been anywhere. However, the movement demonstrated at least some trout were feeding, and feeding not far from the surface.

These sporadic signs of fish kept us going longer than we would have otherwise, because takes were few and far between. We finally left the lake around midday having landed a single modest brown, and having missed just a couple of others. I departed with the uneasy feeling that we hadn't done Tantangara justice. Had we overlooked a killing fly; had we fished too deep or not deep enough? Or (heaven forbid) had we given up too soon, just before some subtle change in temperature or light had launched the trout into an invisible frenzy? These and other questions nag the unsuccessful blind fisher — by definition, you just don't know.

An afternoon session at Eucumbene was equally cryptic. Hardly any fish moved, and rich beds of yabbies and mudeyes, where logic suggested the trout should be feeding, produced precious few takes.

We went back to Lake Jindabyne the next day. I don't want to play favourites between three major Snowy lakes, but Jindabyne is certainly hard to beat as a blind-fishing venue. For a start the shoreline weaves like a lost parrot, creating an endless series of cosy bays and secretive corners. There are monument-sized boulders, drop-offs and shallows, silt flats and weedbeds, beaches of pure sand and messy clusters of drowned trees. The water covering these features is always clear and it is often possible to make out a mysterious log or looming rock more than 2 metres below the surface.

The promising appearance of Lake Jindabyne alone should inspire the doubtful blind fisher, but if one is still wavering, consideration of its robust trout population offers further comfort. In addition to excellent natural spawning facilities, Gaden Trout Hatchery is a modest jog from the shore, feeding the lake with tens of thousands of wild-bred juvenile rainbows each year, not to mention brook trout and even Atlantic salmon. In short, Lake Jindabyne looks as if it should hold lots of trout, and it does.

Having all the parts present never guarantees success, and Trevor and I blanked at Creel Bay that morning. The fish were there all right, sporadically splashing and bow-waving in the sun-dappled ripple. A couple of trout porpoised slowly enough to confirm they were very big: a foot at least between tail and dorsal. As per the previous day, we never actually managed to cover a sighted fish — as in land the fly in front of one within a second or two of seeing it — but we knew they were in the area.

I missed three takes. Two were just bumps down deep that didn't hook up. What can you do? However the third take came after I'd weighted the tippet with tungsten putty and let my Assassin fly sink deeper than usual. The fly was taken hard on the first strip and in my surprise I let the line slip. Two metres of plastic-coated string shot past my groping fingers before I regained control, and by then it was too late. Damn.

At first glance, the morning could be seen as vindication for those who choose not to fish blind: hours of casting and not a fish to hand. However, the feeling I was left with wasn't one of futility or boredom, but rather of a problem yet to be solved. As Trevor and I ate rapidly cooling meat pies on the tailgate of his ute, the conversation was excited and positive, notwithstanding the reflux I experienced every time I recalled *that* missed take. The fish were there, we agreed, and they had to be catchable. So where to next? And what method to try?

Following lunch we decided on a bay we'd fished together months earlier, and after a bit of a walk down a steep timbered spur we reached the water. Although fish disturbed the surface less regularly than at Creel Bay, this more remote part of the lake felt every bit as good, maybe better. Why was that I wondered? Trevor was clearly just as taken with the new spot, striding purposefully toward a pretty corner where a relatively shallow shore merged with a steeper one. He stripped line off and began casting with the controlled urgency of someone who's seen a good fish — except he hadn't, other than perhaps in his mind's eye.

The first trout swiped at Trevor's grizzle-hackled Woolly Bugger as he lifted off to recast, but missed — apparently a big brown of 5 pounds or more. The next bit of action was Trevor's too; a smaller brown this time of 2 pounds or so, but notable for being the first trout actually landed for the day. Whatever made Trevor decide to fish where he was fishing, it was clearly an inspired choice. I liked my own spot where a shallower margin dropped into oblivion about 5 metres out from shore, but with every unmolested cast, I thought more about the bay I knew lay hidden on the other side of the spur.

Eventually I left and headed over to the hidden bay on my own — nothing was going to move Trevor! I took off the loyal Assassin and changed to one of Muz Wilson's Emu Woolly Buggers. The fly was large and very green — perhaps too much for a bright day? Yet it wriggled and pulsed with a life of its own as I test-swam it against the bank. Two kangaroos looked on vacantly, torn I imagined between the quality of the lakeside grass, and a distantly remembered fear of man.

The lake margin sank steadily away here rather than dramatically. The weedbeds were more luxuriant though, and the offshore breeze left a broad strip of the bay flat calm. It was only mid afternoon, yet already the far side of the bay was in the shadows of the steep mountainside beyond.

I cast the Woolly Bugger about 20 metres straight out, then let the fly settle, relying on the weight of the heavy-gauge size 6 hook to pull it slowly down. After about ten seconds I began to retrieve the fly, twisting the line with my left hand in a slow gathering retrieve. It was gloriously quiet in the amphitheatre of the bay, the only sounds being the breeze-rustled treetops on the spur, and the lazy thump-thump of the kangaroos as they hopped from one seemingly identical patch of grass to another. The kangaroos barely looked my way now as they grazed and scratched their chests — evidently I was already accepted as a harmless creature, strangely obsessed with the lake and little else.

And I was obsessed, or at least very taken by this spot. Several casts passed without event and not a fish moved. Yet I felt every tremor of the line through my fingers and I watched its thin trail of pale green religiously.

The Woolly Bugger crept unseen towards me, then just short of the outer edge of the weedbed, the line between my rod tip and the water leapt like a startled snake. This time my fingers didn't slip. As I lifted the rod, the fish was already hooked, pulling out and down.

At this moment, the blind fisher has one over the sight fisher: the thrill of not knowing exactly what has been hooked. For seconds at least and sometimes minutes, the force at the other end of the line is invisible. Is it a maiden rainbow, a ball of silver muscle fighting above its weight division? Or could it be a giant brown, slow to anger and merely contemptuous (so far) of the resistance your line is applying?

The trout moved further out into the lake, then swung to the right, drawing the line in a wide arc. There were a few emergent sticks down that way, and I turned the rod on its side and tried to lever the fish back my way. I succeeded, and for the first time the trout came to the surface — in fact, it shot through it and hung in the air for a long second. Well, it wasn't a monster, but a nice brown all the same.

It took a couple more minutes to bring the trout to the net and confirm its weight at not quite 4 pounds. It was a lovely young fish, small headed and thick bodied. It changed from bronze to almost silver depending on which way I tilted it in the late-afternoon light.

From then on I could do no wrong. Within fifteen minutes I hooked another slightly smaller brown as I searched the weedy edge a bit further down the shore. Soon after landing that fish, the barest hesitation in the line alerted me to another possible take, and I struck into a large rainbow. That trout cartwheeled and pirouetted across the lake until the hook eventually came out, but it didn't really matter.

Blind fishing hardly seemed the right term to describe what I was doing now. I couldn't actually see the trout (besides those I hooked) but I could sense them. I knew the fish were there, just as I know cold air lies on the outside of a cabin window on a winter night. Later I would wonder exactly what it is that enables the blind fisher to achieve this state, where you find yourself fishing with the same anticipation you feel when covering sighted trout.

Wondering could wait however. There were more fish to be caught, and as the remainder of the bay filled with the shadow of the mountain, it looked even better. Trevor turned up around then. He'd caught a couple more fish at his spot, he reported, but was now looking for an offshore breeze for evening. I gestured back to the left where I'd landed the two fish earlier, then added, 'But it all looks good.'

'Does, doesn't it?' responded Trevor thoughtfully as his gaze swept the bay, then he strode purposefully in the direction I'd suggested.

The blind fishing ended soon after that. When the false sunset created by the topography was followed by the real thing, fish started to swirl and porpoise over a wide area of the bay. As is so often the case on late-autumn evenings, the activity seemed disproportionate to the meagre ration of tiny caddis and even tinier midge that we could see. Not that it was a frantic rise (this late in autumn they rarely are) but it was steady and some individual trout moved twice or three times in succession, enabling Trevor and I to judge their speed and direction. Before I knew it, we were really sight fishing, staring into gloom for rises, then placing the fly (the only change I made was replacing the green Woolly for a black one) in the right spot as quickly as possible. Often enough we'd get it right. Land the fly ... pause for a second ... slow strip ... strip again ... yank! Sometimes there was a yell of victory as the hook-up proved solid, sometimes an expletive as the fish got off — although given our successes to that point, these were usually followed by a chuckle rather than a despairing moan.

After half an hour of this, the light had faded to a point where we were hearing most rises before we saw them. We fished on, but the notorious Snowy Mountains chill was descending over the lake with its usual speed. As I picked some weed off the hook of my Woolly Bugger in the torchlight, I noticed my breath was steaming. For the first time in several hours, the shore of Lake Jindabyne wasn't the best place I could think of being. From somewhere along the shore, I could hear Trevor winding in, and I knew he felt the same.

I'd been back home from the Snowys for a couple of weeks when Christopher arrived from Tasmania as the last of autumn turned to true winter. Chris is one of the most accomplished anglers I've fished with, not to mention a highly regarded professional guide. And unlike some guides, he can't wait to go fishing when he's not working. During the off season, he crams everything from bluefin tuna to the tropics to trout in the northern hemisphere into an itinerary that would look exhausting — if it wasn't devoted to catching fish on the fly.

A few months earlier I had been fishing with Christopher in Tasmania, at first embarrassing myself with a few typical guided guide stuff-ups, then settling into the trip and catching plenty of nice trout. One evening, following a particularly fine day on the gum beetles, the talk turned to off-season opportunities. Flushed with the confidence a successful day can bring, I recklessly mentioned that although the streams in my home state of Victoria were closed over winter, there was some fine lake fishing on offer then.

That was true — sort of. As I sipped a beer while we waited for some steaks to sizzle on the other side, I told Chris about lightly rippled winter afternoons when smelters crashed shoreline baitfish like miniature killer whales, or when midge feeders cruised gracefully, fins and backs creasing the steely water. After a thoughtful pause I added that when the winter sun shines, it's remarkable how many big trout can be polaroided cruising the banks. No wonder Chris jumped at the chance to join me for a couple of days in June.

When planning for Chris's visit, I decided the best idea was to take him to the twin volcanic lakes of Bullen Merri and Purrumbete. My reasons were fourfold. First, these lakes are unique, so at the very least he'd be fishing water unlike anything he'd seen before, and pretty water at that. Second, the trout and salmon are usually beauties, so if he did catch a fish, I wouldn't be embarrassed by its size. Third, there was a fair chance he might land a chinook salmon, one of the few species of fish he hadn't caught on the fly. Finally — and I know I was tempting fate to even think this — I hadn't actually blanked down on those lakes for several trips.

The appointed day dawned cold and windy. I don't mind flogging the rough stuff at Bullen Merri or Purrumbete on my own (the fish can actually take better), but you don't see as many fish. Oh well, those were the conditions we'd been dealt.

We were just about blown over by the gale that hit us as we climbed over the eastern crater rim at Purrumbete, but fortunately the wind abated somewhat as we descended to water level. It was possible to cast out past the onshore waves. Beyond the churned up shoreline the water was clear. When a fleeting patch of sun lit the area around us, Chris called out from his waist-deep position that the lake looked 'bloody good!' It did too. Clumps of weed swayed beneath the waves like drowned bonsai growing up from a bed of pale sand and silt. It was easy to picture a big trout or chinook salmon slicing through this aquatic savannah, ambushing any galaxias or gudgeon caught in the open.

The water looked so fishy that, even after an hour of nothing, Chris was still fishing as if a take was imminent, casting with purpose and tilting his head this way and that for a better look. Watching him continue to search so purposefully, on foreign water where he was yet to see a single fish, reinforced the sort of angler Chris is.

Two hours and still nothing, then just as I was about to suggest a move to Bullen Merri, a huge brown swam right past my feet, its greenish-gold shape glowing against the dark weed along the drop-off. I'd just cast my Yeti 20 metres away, and by the time I retrieved and was ready to cover the shape, it had gone. A little later, a good fish swirled right inshore among the stones, but I was too slow to pick it as a trout. Once again I ended up casting to where the fish might have gone instead of to where it was.

Those two sightings kept us working Purrumbete with renewed enthusiasm for another hour. During that time, I might have had a single hit but I couldn't be sure. On my own I would have stayed, but Chris hadn't seen or felt a fish and I decided the mere potential for action was no longer enough. We reeled in and walked the long sandy shore back to the crater rim and the car.

Bullen Merri looked good as it nearly always does. Even driving down the long steep slope above the north shore, I could make out the pale perimeter flats and how they ended at the plunging drop-off for which this clover-shaped volcanic lake is famous.

I pointed out various features as we descended into the crater — the 'coral' on the north shore where some friends and I once landed several good salmon and a trout on a single sunny afternoon; the bay to the left of Potters Point where I heartbreakingly lost a giant chinook at the net; the drop-off just beyond the western flats where a mate landed an 11-pound rainbow. I think I was trying to encourage myself as much as Chris.

All shores except the western shore were chopped by a steady wave, and because by this stage I wanted Chris to at least see a fish, the calm western bays were the obvious choice.

Literally as we pulled up in the car, a large fish swirled violently only 10 metres from the bank. In no time we were both down at the water, casting Woolly Buggers in the general direction of the activity, hunched like loaded springs. Every ten minutes or so a fish would move somewhere within sight, and mostly right along the drop-off. It was hardly a frenzy but at least we knew feeding fish were in the area. Many looked like big ones.

Another hour went by. I had one solid bump, but still nothing for Chris. Being mid June, the day was running out fast and already our shadows were long enough to force us to stand well back from the drop-off. It was time to try another spot, so we jumped in the car and headed for my favourite location on the north shore, unfriendly wind or not. In the event the spot looked good and the wave wasn't as bad as I thought it would be. More fishing, more casts, but nothing for either of us. No takes, no swirls.

Chris wandered back to the car before me, and by the time I joined him he was already enjoying a coffee on the tailgate and watching the crater walls turn from orange to dull pink. He looked like he'd finished fishing for the day. I gave my final pitch. 'Half an hour 'til dark mate, the best time of day. Let's give the western shore one more go.' It was more a plea than a suggestion.

We headed hastily back to the area where we'd seen the fish. 'Okay Chris, stand right there,' I insisted, pointing to the spot I judged to be most central to the activity we'd witnessed earlier, although nothing at all was moving now. I added ironically, 'You can't miss!' Chris laughed (at least he still had a sense of humour) and began casting. Second blind cast, his rod tip lurched down and his reel began to whirr. A few moments later, a large fish sloshed on the surface. It was a dogged, powerful fight. After the fish had bulldozed off on one particularly strong run, Chris suddenly announced, 'S#@t! I think I'm still on 4-pound tippet!' I groaned, but unclipped my landing net anyway. By the time the fish came within net range, there was just enough daylight left to operate without the torch. I saw one good shot as it came over the lip of the drop-off, and I scooped up a heavy, thrashing trout. It was a brown trout and it weighed 7 pounds.

A few casts later I missed my best take of the day. I cursed with suitable enthusiasm, but to tell the truth I didn't really mind.